The Book Writer

Other Allison & Busby Writers' Guides:

Gordon Wells

The Book Writer's Handbook

Second, Revised, Edition

ALLISON & BUSBY

An Allison & Busby book
Published in 1991 by
Virgin Books Plc
26 Grand Union Centre,
338 Ladbroke Grove,
London W10 5AH

First published by Allison & Busby 1989
Second edition published 1991

Set in Linotron Times by Intype, London
Printed and bound in Great Britain by
Mackays of Chatham PLC, Chatham, Kent

ISBN 0 85031 813 0

The moral right of the author has been asserted

CONTENTS

Introduction

You're writing a book? That's great. Have you thought about a publisher yet? You will need to, fairly soon; and that is what this book is all about; finding **the right publisher**.

Whether you are writing a first novel, a biography of Nefertiti, or a book on how to crochet beer-mats, you still have to find yourself a publisher. And different publishers often have different requirements — which may affect the way you need to write. This is not something confined just to non-fiction writing either; the preferred length of a romantic novel for Robert Hale is 45,000 words; the preferred length of a romantic novel for Mills & Boon is 50–55,000 words. If it's right for one, it's wrong for the other.

One non-fiction publisher of "how to" books will want a 35,000-word book with lots of examples, lists, tables, etc. — another may prefer a much longer book with diagrammatic illustrations only. Many non-fiction publishers will want your book to fit into an existing series. You need to find all this sort of thing out, before you put in too much abortive effort.

A beginning fiction writer may blithely assume that he or she will get an agent to deal with finding a publisher; but getting an agent to take you on can be as hard as finding a publisher to accept your work. A first-time non-fiction writer will find it almost impossible to get an agent — and often has little need for one.

No. No one will do this work for you. For your first book (and quite possibly for future books too) you have to find your own publisher. And there are hundreds to choose from. If you send a 50,000-word thriller to Northcote House or Gower, you are wasting everyone's time and a lot of postage; similarly, if you send a book on how to crochet beer-mats to New English Library. To choose who shall (first) receive your master-piece, you need to narrow down the field. You need to identify several likely publishers. And that means doing some market research.

Market Research

Around 50,000 new books are published in Britain each year; yet overall, of the thousands of manuscripts that each publisher is offered annually, fewer than 10% are accepted. (The chances of acceptance are markedly greater for a non-fiction book than for a first novel.) To find the "right" publisher entails market research; determining which publisher is likely to be interested in "your" type of book. And judging from the comments of many publishers, far too many writers still submit manuscripts that would be more appropriately submitted — and possibly accepted —

1

elsewhere. This indicates that writers are not doing enough market research.

The "writing business" is not just about writing; it is also about getting the book to the reader. The first step along this path is to sell the manuscript to the right publisher. This, as we have seen, means market research.

Market research of publishers can be done in a variety of ways. The writer can look in the standard reference books; can study the books on shop and library shelves; can ask other writers; or can watch the book reviews in the press.

Each of these methods is valid and has some place in the process. But each, alone, can be rather like sticking a pin in a telephone directory with your eyes closed. One of the standard reference books lists over five hundred British publishers; many entries say little more than that they are interested in "fiction and general non-fiction". No bookshop, or small library can hope to carry books by all of the publishing houses — nor is it their object to do so. Newspaper review pages are extremely selective in what they review; they seldom review much *genre* fiction, for instance. And while individual writers often know their own publisher(s) quite well, they don't always know much about others.

Probably the best method of determining the type of book that a publisher is publishing is to study his catalogue. But there is still the problem of deciding from which publisher the writer should seek a catalogue. You can't look at them all.

This Book

Like its companion volume, *The Magazine Writer's Handbook*, this book is intended to help the (first-time) writer in the choice of publisher. The writer will still need to collect and study a few up-to-date catalogues; will still wish to look, in libraries and shops, at the books published by one or two publishers; will still need to consult other writers for "the scuttlebutt" — the trade gossip. But the field will have been narrowed down.

Even when the choice is narrowed down to just two or three suitable publishers, remember that in any case, the publisher's wants are constantly changing; the new books coming along in the pipeline may well be very different from those already published. Remember too that the first publisher may not accept your book. You need to choose more than one "suitable" publisher.

In selecting the publishers to be reported on in this handbook the very specialist houses were largely excluded. If you are an expert in, say, main-frame computing, you will already know the specialist publishers in this field. Few other writers will be interested in those publishers. If you are an academic, you will probably know of the leading publishers in academic texts who are largely excluded from this book. (But some are included, just for interest.)

Generally too, the smaller, and more localised, publishers are excluded from this handbook. The exception to this is that publishers of poetry are so few that many small houses are included for this reason alone. Along the same lines, the demand — from writers at least — is for publishers for first novels; accordingly, the contents may be slanted, a little more than is otherwise justified, towards the publishers of fiction.

Inevitably though, I shall have left out some publishers who I should not have left out, and included some that I need not have included. No one person's choice can ever be right for everyone's needs.

The material contained in each of the reports which form the bulk of this book comes from a variety of sources. In principle, I have tried to do what any conscientious writer would wish to do, given the time and the opportunities, when selecting a publisher.

I started, as would most writers, by consulting the writer's standard reference book, the *Writers' & Artists' Yearbook*; from that I made my initial choice of publishers. I looked along library, bookshop and my own and others' bookshelves in search of other publishers of possible interest; and I watched the newspapers and magazines for book reviews. (I have followed, as best I could, the media reports on the many changes now under way in the publishing world.) And I made a careful study of the publishers' advertisements in the Spring and Autumn Books issues of *The Bookseller*. (These bumper issues are invaluable for a writer's market research; most public libraries have copies in the reference section.) In many cases, I also obtained copies of publishers' stocklists and new issue catalogues.

Most important of all though, I sent out questionnaires to my chosen publishers. And, although this questionnaire was undoubtedly an unwelcome imposition into already busy lives, most Managing or Editorial Directors completed and returned it. I am most grateful for this assistance. (And once the reports were written, these same busy executives took further time to check the drafts of my reports. Of course, the inevitable residual errors and omissions are still entirely my fault; that there are, hopefully, so few is thanks to the publishers.)

In drafting the reports I have often tried to demonstrate the content of a publisher's list by giving examples of recent titles. My choice of exemplary titles has been purely personal: if I recognized an author's name and his or her book appeared appropriate I mentioned it; if a book title appealed to my sense of humour or sparked my interest, I mentioned it; and I tried to cover the range of titles.

Money

Each of the reports also contains some "hard" information: on the number of fiction and non-fiction books likely to be published each year, on how many of these are from new writers, and which categories of books are published by each publishing house. The reports also contain advice on how different publishers prefer to be approached, on how long it should be before a writer hears the fate of his or her submitted manuscript, and on the likely terms of payment.

Some writers find any discussion of their payment rather embarrassing.

(It is even more embarrassing for them when they find how little they will get for so much work.) Few first-time writers have much idea of the likely terms; they all want to know but some don't like to ask. For that reason, the questionnaire which I sent to publishers asked them to specify the "usual" royalty terms and the likely size of any advance.

Somewhat to my surprise, many publishers were willing to disclose the royalty rates; quite a lot though, declined to specify a minimum advance. This is understandable. Advances are a negotiable amount; they depend on "the book's market potential". The sure-fire best-selling "blockbuster" from a known writer may attract hundreds of thousands of pounds; the "craft" book on how to crochet bed-socks or beer-mats may be lucky to get an advance of £100.

A good rule of thumb for the first-time writer is that the advance is likely to be based on the royalties that would be earned on sales of half the first print run. As an example: a good, but not obviously spectacular, "straight" first novel is to sell at £10 per hardback copy with a royalty rate of 10%, earning the author £1 per copy. A likely first print run is about 2,000 copies. On this basis, the advance might be £1,000. Less would be a bit stingy; to expect more would perhaps be over-optimistic.

Fiction or non-fiction?

One interesting fact to emerge from the questionnaire was the demand — and the opportunities — for non-fiction. Whereas the proportion of first novelists to new fiction was always low, less than 10% overall, at least 50% of all new non-fiction books are by writers coming new to the publisher. And overall, there are four or five times as many new non-fiction books as new novels.

(Against that, of course, the possibility of making a vast amount of money from a non-fiction book is less good than from a novel. A really successful novel can earn a lot from spin-offs — paperback rights, film rights, TV rights, etc. Such extras are seldom open to the biographer or writer of "how to" books.)

Almost all publishers responding to the questionnaire mentioned the need for non-fiction writers to make a thorough appraisal of the need and likely market for their proposed book before putting up the idea. And again and again they stressed the advantages of knowing about competitive books. Non-fiction writers wishing to know just how to submit a proposal for a new book are advised to consult my *The Successful Author's Handbook*, Papermac 2/e 1989.

On the fiction side, whilst several publishers clearly prefer submissions to be "agented" (to be submitted through an agent), almost all accept the virtual impossibility of that for a first-time writer. This is markedly different from practice in the USA where an agent is almost a necessity, even for a new writer.

Another particularly useful piece of advice from the publishers is that they are more likely to buy *genre* fiction than "straight" fiction. For more of the publishers' collected words of advice, as included in the questionnaires returned to me, *see* Chapter 3, page 201.

Elsewhere in the book there are also short chapters on how to submit your work to the publishers, a general miscellany including details on how and where to get together with other writers, a chapter on how to live amicably with a word processor (I couldn't live without one), and lists of which publishers are most likely to be interested in which types of writing.

Finally, it is hoped that this handbook will be reissued at regular intervals. Readers — and publishers — are invited to write to the author, c/o Allison & Busby (at Virgin), with comments or advice on how the book might be improved, or with further information. If a reply is expected, **please send a stamped addressed envelope.**

And, *please* remember; when submitting your work to publishers, *always* send a sufficiently large, adequately stamped, self-addressed envelope.

Changes in this new edition

The British publishing world is in a constant state of flux. Small publishing houses are gobbled up by big conglomerates — or merge with other small firms to become financially viable; large publishers "rationalize" by divesting themselves of less profitable parts of their lists. This new edition of the Handbook reflects these changes.

Several publishers or imprints, included in the First Edition of this Handbook, have been dropped from this edition. Some have ceased operation, some have been absorbed within other imprints, some are reorganising and unable to forecast their future activities. A few will return in later editions. Those dropped are:

> *Burke Publishing Co. Ltd*
> *Canongate Publishing Ltd*
> *Charles Griffin & Co. Ltd*
> *Journeyman Press Ltd*
> *Julia MacRae Books*
> *Frederick Muller*
> *Pagoda Books*
> *Papermac*
> *Unwin Hyman Ltd*
> *Ward Lock Ltd*
> *Wayland (Publishers) Ltd.*

Similarly, several new publishers or imprints have been added, and some, originally shown as part of a "parent" house, now have a page of their own. Those added, are:

> *Business Books*

Element Books
Fourth Estate Ltd
Malvern Publishing Co. Ltd
Optima Books
Piccadilly Press
Serpent's Tail
Simon & Schuster Young Books.

And *W. H. Allen* — the "parent" publishers of this book — are now renamed *Virgin Books* (see page 187).

A new chapter has been added, describing what happens after a book manuscript is delivered to the publisher. Delivery is by no means the end of the story. Yet few first-time authors are aware of the rest of "the process". Chapter 5 will enlighten them.

Additional comments from publishers have been added in Chapter 3; minor updating changes have been made to other chapters. And the "Who Publishes What" tables in Chapter 2 have been completely recast, taking account of the revised information in Chapter 1.

Chapter 1 has been almost totally rewritten, incorporating up-to-date book titles, up-dated expectations of the number of new publications, changes in terms, requirements etc. The statistical information — number of books published, etc. — at the top of each page has been extended to show the number of fiction and non-fiction titles in print. This gives an indication of the publisher's size.

As before, the draft reports were shown to each publisher before the book went to print; they had the opportunity to correct inaccuracies. As before, I am grateful for this considerable assistance by busy editorial directors and their staff. The improved accuracy is thanks to them, the responsibility for residual errors is mine.

1

The Publishers

This long chapter contains the real meat of this book: the detailed reports on each of the selected publishers.

Each report is in a common format, each on its own page. Factual information — publisher, address and phone number and where possible, the persons to whom submissions should be addressed — is at the top; beneath that there is a review of the publisher's interests and list exemplified by a number of recent titles, also, any advice such as maximum book lengths, etc.; at the foot of the page there is advice on how each publisher prefers work to be submitted, how long it should take to get a decision, and how much you might expect to be paid.

At the top right corner of each page is a box, with "statistical" information. The key — and an example — are overleaf.

F: Fiction: Number of new titles/year — say 1990
          (Of new titles, number of first novels)
          Total number of titles currently in print

Fiction categories:

G: General	L: "Literary"	R: Romance
C: Crime/thriller	S: sci-fi/fantasy	W: Western
K: Childrens	Poetry .... P at right margin	

NF: Non-fiction: Number of new titles/year — say 1990
          (Of those, number by authors *new to publisher*)
          Total number of NF titles in print

Non-fiction categories:

1: history/biography/royalty	2: travel/nature
3: gen. interest/art/antiques	4: crafts/how-to/DIY
5: hobbies and sports	6: management
7: academic/specialist tech.	8: educational
Humour .... H at right margin	

All numbers, and the basis of the categorisation, are as provided by the publishers.

Example

Taking the immediately adjacent Allison & Busby entry as an example, the "box" shows:

F: 25 (3)	75
[L, G, C]	
NF: 15 (3)	50
[1, 3, 4]	

That is, Allison & Busby currently (1990) publish 25 fiction titles per year, of which 3 were first novels; they have 75 fiction titles in print. They publish "literary", general and crime novels. Similarly, they publish 15 non-fiction books per year, of which 3 were by authors new to Allison & Busby, and altogether, there are 50 titles in print. Their non-fiction interests are: history, biography (and royalty); general interest, art and antiques; and books on crafts (these Writers' Guides, for example), hobbies and DIY. Book proposals should be addressed to the Editorial Director, Peter Day.

NOTE: W. H. Allen is now Virgin Publishing — see page 187

ALLISON & BUSBY

Subsidiary of Virgin Publishing
338 Ladbroke Grove
London W10 5AH

T: 081–968 7554

F: 25 (3)	75
[L, G, C]	
NF: 15 (3)	50
[1, 3, 4]	

Fiction and non-fiction: Peter Day (Editorial Director)

Allison & Busby, which publishes prestigious and radical titles, is a subsidiary of Virgin Publishing (which used to be W. H. Allen) — see page 187.

The Allison & Busby backlist consists of about two-thirds fiction and one-third non-fiction; new titles are published in approximately the same proportions. It publishes roughly a dozen hardbacks and two dozen paperbacks a year.

Fiction authors in the backlist include such greats as Colin MacInnes (*Absolute Beginners*), Boris Pasternak, and J. B. Priestley. There is a strong American crime list with titles by Ross Macdonald, Richard Stark, Donald Westlake and Chester Himes.

Recent additions to the fiction list include two first novels, *Lives of the Saints* by Nino Ricci and *The Children Who Sleep by the River* by Debbie Taylor. There are also several new books in the American Crime series.

The non-fiction list is in two parts. The general section has had a number of big successes, including the cult management book *A Book of Five Rings* by Miyamoto Musashi in translation by Victor Harris. Other prestigious authors include the socio-political writer C. L. R. James and the biographers Henri Troyat, Philip Callow, and Joanna Cullen Brown.

The second part of the non-fiction list contains the twenty or so paperbacks in the successful Writers' Guides series (*see* page 187) — of which this book is one. It is hoped to publish about three new Writers' Guides a year.

Editorial Director Peter Day is ". . . always looking for quality books, either fiction or non-fiction."

Initial approach: For both fiction and non-fiction, Peter Day likes a clear statement of the theme of a book and a short but clear synopsis first. Thereafter, two sample chapters. He does not like *obvious* dot-matrix printing.
Decisions: out-and-out rejections usually come within a week; firm acceptances can take longer (maybe 2 months) — there are a lot of "maybes" in the process.
Terms: standard 10% on hardbacks, 7.5% on paperbacks, on list price, paid twice annually. Advances are variable but "reasonable".

ANGUS & ROBERTSON (UK) LTD

Division of HarperCollins Publishers
77–85 Fulham Palace Road,
London W6 8JB

T: 081–741 7070

F: 10 (0)	20
[L, C]	
NF: 50 (25)	200
[1, 3, 4]	H

Fiction: NIL (almost invariably Australian only)
Non-fiction: Valerie Hudson (Editorial Director)

The UK branch of a major Australian publisher which was founded over a hundred years ago, Angus & Robertson (UK) has a small, select list of books. (There are about 200 titles in their current stock list, of which 90% is non-fiction.) Virtually all their fiction is of Australian origin (notably Arthur Upfield's *Inspector Bonaparte* mysteries); they are not interested in seeing novels from British writers — despite which they are offered over 500 novel manuscripts each year. On the non-fiction side though, they welcome British submissions; they are offered around 1,000 a year — and take about 1%.

The Angus & Robertson (UK) non-fiction list is particularly strong in humorous books and cookery books.

Their titles help to give a "feel" of the Angus & Robertson (UK) humorous books. There are: *Business Widows: A Handbook for Workaholics* by Noel Ford; *Wicked French* and *Wicked Italian*, both by Howard Tomb; and *Great Lies: The Ultimate Fibber's Handbook* by Jo Donnelly. They also have an ongoing series, *The World's Best . . . Jokes* which already includes Aussie, Catholic, Irish, Holiday, Lawyer . . . you name it.

Angus & Robertson (UK) also publish more general non-fiction books. Recent titles have included *Topping* — the autobiography of the police chief in the Moors murder case; *Eat Green — Lose Weight* by Dr Vernon Coleman; and *Prisoner: Cell Block H — Behind the Scenes* by Terry Bourke. Not surprisingly, there are books on Australian wine, Australian travel — and Australian cricket — too.

Initial approach: as above, no fiction. For non-fiction, they prefer approaches through an agent. However submitted, they always want a detailed synopsis, a review of the need for the book, and its competitors, and the author's credentials.
Decisions: usually within about a month.
Terms: royalties usually 10% on hardback and 7.5% on paperback list price UK sales. Advances can be up to £5,000; very often less. (But £750 minimum.)

ANVIL PRESS POETRY

Poetry: 17 (9*)   200
* = new only to Anvil

69 King George Street,
London SE10 8PX

T: 081–858 2946

Poetry: Julia Sterland and Peter Jay (Editors)

Founded in 1968 as a specialist publisher of poetry only, Anvil Press Poetry are offered far more unsolicited poetry than they can possibly cope with — around 300 possible books per year. And much of their material is selected anyway, from abroad, in translation.

They say, very frankly, "It would be perverse to have a policy of not accepting unsolicited manuscripts, since a few very good poets whom we publish have reached us in just this way. So, we *do* consider everything that comes through the letter box. That said, I'm afraid that almost everything that arrives ends up being returned — including perfectly publishable material, and the odd manuscript that we would dearly *like* to publish."

Among recent poetry books published by Anvil are *A Selection of Poems* by John Birtwhistle, Peter Levi's *Shadow and Bone*, and Philip Sherrard's *In the Sign of the Rainbow*. In translation, they have recently offered *The August Sleepwalker* by Bei Dao, the young Chinese poet, and *The Selected Poems of Vittorio Sereni*. Their list also includes a number of anthologies — recently, *The Poetry of Survival* edited by Daniel Weissbort.

As specialist publishers, with limited resources, Anvil have only a small staff — not more than two or three altogether. They point out that this means that they are often slow in dealing with unsolicited material.

Initial approach: try submitting just a sample — at least it keeps down the bulk and the cost of postage.
Decisions: can take more than three months.
Terms: for work which is accepted, Anvil Press Poetry pay royalties of 10% on list price for domestic sales and 10% of net receipts for overseas sales. An advance of up to £150 is possible.

Anvil Press acknowledges the financial assistance of the Arts Council of Great Britain.

ARROW BOOKS (incl VINTAGE and RED FOX)

F: 730 (?)	1450
[all]	
NF: 240 (?)	670
[1–4, 6]	H

Division of The Random Century
Group Ltd
Random Century House,
20 Vauxhall Bridge Road,
London SW1V 2SA

T: 071–973–9700

Fiction and non-fiction: Simon Master (Man. Dir.)
Children's Books — Red Fox: Alison Berry
Vintage: Frances Coady (Editorial Director)

Arrow Books are the mass-market paperback wing of The Random Century Group. They publish all types and genres of fiction including, in the Red Fox imprint, books for young and teenaged children. They also publish popular non-fiction.

Their backlist includes such famous names as Dennis Wheatley ("Black" thrillers) and P. G. Wodehouse (*Jeeves*, etc.). Today, their authors include — under her own name — the joint "Queen of Crime", Ruth Rendell (the other "Queen" being P. D. James, of course) with her many suspense and crime titles. One of her most recent Arrow titles is *The Bridesmaid*, a psychological suspense novel. Other big name fiction writers in the Arrow list include Fay Weldon, Colleen McCullough, William Horwood (*The Duncton Chronicles*) and Brian Moore.

The Arrow non-fiction list is broad-based: it ranges across such titles as Tony Benn's *Diaries*, *The Complete Speaker's Handbook* by Bob Monkhouse, *Driven to Win* by Nigel Mansell, and Tim Severin's *The Jason Voyage*. There are also "fitness" and humorous books.

Vintage is a newly launched up-market list, concentrating on publishing international authors of distinction in paperback. Early titles include *Sexing the Cherry* by Jeanette Winterson, *Deception* by Philip Roth, and *Possession* by A. S. Byatt.

Children's books, from the new imprint, Red Fox, include picture books, activity and joke books (including the bestselling *How to Handle Grown-Ups*), poetry (from such writers as Gavin Ewart and Colin West) and fiction from, among others, Jean Ure, Colin Dann.

Initial approach: Arrow are not enthusiastic about receiving ANY unsolicited manuscripts — but they still receive around twenty each week. If you feel you must try them, for both fiction and non-fiction, Arrow prefer to receive a written query to ascertain their likely interest, before any actual manuscripts are submitted.
Decisions: usually within no more than one month.
Terms: Arrow are not prepared to give details of terms.

BANTAM PRESS

Division of Transworld Publishers Ltd
61–63 Uxbridge Road, London W5 5SA

T: 081–579 2652

F: 55 (3)	...
[L, G, C, S]	
NF: 45 (40)	...
[1–6 incl]	H

Fiction and non-fiction: Ursula Mackenzie (Editorial Director)

A division of the Transworld organisation — best-known perhaps for its Corgi and other paperbacks (*See* page 51) — Bantam Press is a hardback publishing house dividing its interests roughly 55%/45% fiction/non-fiction.

The fiction is mainly "general popular" — epitomised by such titles as Sally Beauman's much-hyped *Destiny*, and Jilly Cooper's sex-romps *Riders* and *Rivals*. Recent titles of a like nature include *Sex In The Afternoon* by June Flaum Singer and *Dazzle* by Judith Krantz. But Bantam also have a lot of other big bestselling authors too. Recent slightly less flamboyant titles include the latest Catherine Cookson, *The Gillyvors*, a new Anne McCaffrey, *The Renegades of Pern*, and *Well-Schooled in Murder*, an Inspector Lynley story, by Elizabeth George.

The non-fiction list is strong on biography and general popular non-fiction. Recent titles include *A Damned Serious Business: My Life in Comedy* by Rex Harrison, *Hunting Marco Polo: The Pursuit and Capture of Howard Marks* by Paul Eddy and Sara Walden, and *Enslaved: An Investigation into Modern-day Slavery* by Gordon Thomas. On the "business-anecdotal" side there is *Father, Son & Company: My Life at IBM and Beyond* by Thomas J. Watson Jr. and Peter Petre. And there is *Mind Magic* by Betty Shine.

Initial approach: fiction — a marked preference for submissions through an agent. If no agent, write in with a descriptive query letter first — don't just send a fiction manuscript in on spec. For non-fiction, the usual package of synopsis, justification, credentials and two sample chapters — and in this case, direct submission is more acceptable.
Decisions: can take three months.
Terms: for first-time writers, royalties usually 10%/7.5% hb/pb on home sales at list price. Advances vary with potential, but can be £1,000 plus.

B. T. BATSFORD LTD

4 Fitzhardinge Street,
London W1H 0AH

T: 071–486 8484

F: NIL
NF: 125 (60)   1300
[1, 3–8 incl]

Non-fiction: Timothy Auger (Editorial Director)

Batsford, established 1843, started publishing in 1874 (before that, they were in bookselling) and have built up a big reputation, and a big backlist. They publish only non-fiction and tend to specialise in craft and "pastime" books; they are very strong on books about chess. But they publish a good general non-fiction list — the specialisms are strengths within it.

Within the general list, they have recently launched a major new series with English Heritage, including *Hadrian's Wall* by Stephen Johnson, *Avebury* by Caroline Malone, and *Church Archaeology* by Warwick Rodwell. They are also strong on fashion books (eg *Christian Dior* by Diana de Marly) and books on equestrian and other country sports. Another recent title, *The Larger Rhododendron Species* by Peter Cox, exemplifies the Batsford philosophy of identifying a specialist interest and commissioning a leading authority to write about it.

The craft list is equally good and very specific. Among recent titles are *Chinese Painting: The Complete Self Tutor* by Francisca Ting, *Pattern on the Knitting Machine* by Ruth Lee, and *The Sampler Quilt Workbook* by Dinah Travis. If you are really expert at almost any craft, Batsford might be interested in a book about it. (Probably a second book about it; there can be few skills or craft activities that they do not already cover.) The emphasis is on established crafts entailing considerable expertise.

They publish many books about chess. These range from popular guides, to studies of the great players and of various openings. Typical of recent titles is *Batsford Chess Openings 2* by Ray Keene and Gary Kasparov.

Batsford also publish technical and school library books. Their Mitchell's series of building textbooks lead the field; there is also a growing list of illustrated titles aimed at architects and designers. And there are such major tomes as *The Batsford Book of English Poetry* and *The Feminist Companion to Literature in English*.

Initial approach: detailed synopsis, assessment of need, market and competition, and statement of author's credentials. Sample chapters should be ready to follow.
Decisions: can take three months, but usually much less.
Terms: Vary — they will not generalise.

BLACKIE CHILDREN'S BOOKS

Imprint of Blackie & Son Ltd, Glasgow
7 Leicester Place, London WC2H 7BP
T: 071–734 7521

F: 90 (30)	300
[K]	P
NF: NIL	

Fiction (and poetry): Martin West (Children's Publisher)

Blackie Children's Books is part of the Blackie Publishing Group; Blackie were founded as far back as 1809 — and even today are still independent. The separate children's imprint was set up within the last few years.

They publish a wide range of novelty, board and picture books: board books include Rodney Peppe's ABC alphabet book; novelties include soft books and bath books; and there is a wide range of picture books with authors such as Val Biro, Prue Theobalds and Shoo Rayner. And then there are the *Topsy and Tim* books — around 150 of them, by Jean and Gareth Adamson.

Of more interest to the budding writer, though, are the wordier books. First there is the Blackie Bears series, for first readers: 48-page books, such as Pamela Oldfield's *A Shaggy Dog Story* and Michael Hardcastle's *Joanna's Goal*. Next comes the Fiction for Younger Readers series (for 9–11 year olds) with such titles as Morris Gleitzman's *Poms* and Chris Powling's *Dracula in Sunlight*. This series also includes the winner of the 1989 Kathleen Fidler Award (see below), Clare Bevan's *Mightier than the Sword*.

There is a new fiction series for 8–10 year old readers, called "Blackie Snappers". These are contemporary, humorous stories such as *Jeffrey's Joke Machine* by Alexander McCall Smith and *Playing With Fire* by Anthony Masters. Another series for the 8–10s is "Thriller Firsts" — stories of action and suspense; recent titles include David Wiseman's *Moonglow* and Jon Blake's *Roboskool*.

Blackie also has a new series of contemporary stories "full of magic, humour and adventure" for 6–8 year olds, called "Story Factory". Early titles include *Griselda FGM* by Margaret Ryan, and Alexander McCall Smith's *Marzipan Max*.

Then there is the "Fiction for Older Readers" list for readers aged 10+; this includes *Stormsearch* by Robert Westall and *The Great Sandwich Racket and other stories* by Andrew Matthews.

Blackie publish a limited amount of poetry for children. This is usually only anthologies, but they *are* willing to look at original work if accurately aimed at children under 14.

Blackie Children's Books are keen to encourage new writers for children. They do this in a positive way by sponsoring the annual Kathleen Fidler Award, which was set up in 1980 and is adminstered by the Book Trust Scotland. Both new authors, and established authors new to writing for the 8–12 age group, of any nationality, may submit work for the Award. The requirement is a work of fiction for the 8–12 age group, not exceeding 30,000 words in length, properly presented (see page 206); the prize is £1,000, a handsome trophy, and an option for Blackie to publish the winning entry. (Each winner so far has been published by Blackie with great success.)

At the present time, entries have to be sent to The Kathleen Fidler Award, c/o Book Trust Scotland, 15a Lynedoch Street, Glasgow G3 6EF, to reach them by 31 October. Further details, if required, may be obtained from the Book Trust Scotland by writing as above, or by phoning 041–332 0391; or by phoning Blackie Children's Books, Martin West, on 071–734 7521.

Initial approach: other than for the Kathleen Fidler Award, Blackie prefer to see just the first two chapters of a novel together with a synopsis of the rest.

Decisions: because of the huge number of unsolicited manuscripts they receive — about 1,000 each year — decisions can take two to three months.

Terms: royalties of 7.5% on home hardback sales based on the published price are paid. Advance for a children's novel would probably be around £500.

BLOODAXE BOOKS LTD

P.O. Box 1SN,
Newcastle upon Tyne NE99 1SN

T: 091–232 5988

F: 1 (1)	6
NF*: 24 (15)	P
* mostly poetry	160
[and 1, 3, drama]	

All: Andrew McAllister (Assistant Editor)

Founded in 1978, Bloodaxe Books is a small and lively specialist publisher. Supported loyally by Northern Arts, they are undoubtedly "Number One" in Britain for new poetry. But they also publish a few other books; their list, which contains around 170 titles in all, includes only about 20 "non-poetry" books. There are four books of photographs, a handful of fiction, some drama and some literary non-fiction.

Bloodaxe do not expect to publish any fiction in the near future — but they will look at possibilities.

It is for poetry though that Bloodaxe are best known. Recent titles include *The Heart, The Border*, a collection of powerful poems about the Berlin Wall by Ken Smith, once writer-in-residence at Wormwood Scrubs. Other titles to catch my eye include *Counterpoint* by religious poet R. S. Thomas, John Greening's *Tutankhamun Variations*, and the selected poems of Dorothy Hewett (*see also* Virago, page 185), *Alice in Wormland*.

Their one recent novel was a first, a working-class story, *Kiddar's Luck* by Tyneside author, Jack Common. One of their few recent general non-fiction books was *Under the Rainbow*, a handbook by David Morley.

In an average year they receive over 3,000 unsolicited manuscripts which, remembering how few new titles they publish each year, shows their perceived importance. "And yet," they say, "most of the poetry submissions sent to us are completely unsuitable for our list. It would save everyone's time if the author were to *read* some of our books first, to see what kind of work we publish." In literary criticism and biography, they are "interested in seeing books which relate literature to a wider social and political context."

Initial approach: fiction and non-fiction, try a query first; poetry, a dozen poems as a sample and an indication of what else is available. But read their poetry books first — Constance Spry or Pam Ayres they're not.
Decisions: can take three months.
Terms: royalties usually 10% hb and pb home sales and 7.5% on all overseas sales. Advances vary with the book's likely potential.

BLOOMSBURY PUBLISHING LTD

2 Soho Square, London W1V 5DE

T: 071–494 2111

F: 43 (12)	115
[L, C]	
NF: 117 (?)	310
[1, 2, 3, 4, 5, 6]	H

Fiction: Editorial Dept. — Cory McCracken
Non-fiction: Editorial Dept. — Rachel King

Founded in 1986, Bloomsbury is now well established as an independent publisher, and it is building up its list fast. Interestingly, it awards equity shares in the company to its authors.

Bloomsbury is — numerically, at least — stronger in non-fiction than in fiction. But the fiction list, avowedly "literary" under the control of Liz Calder, one of the better editors around, is certainly not negligible. Recent titles include *My Son's Story* by Nadine Gordimer, *The Other Side* by Mary Gordon, *Sexing the Cherry* by Jeanette Winterson, *This is What Happens When You Don't Pay Attention* by David Holden and *Maestro* by Peter Goldsworthy.

The non-fiction side of Bloomsbury is strong on reference books; recent titles here include Tony Thorne's *Bloomsbury Dictionary of Contemporary Slang* and Leo and Herman Schneider's *Dictionary of Science for Everyone*. Recent non-reference books range from *Linda McCartney's Home Cooking* by Linda McCartney and Peter Cox, through Patrick Skene Catling's *The Joy of Freeloading* and Paula Yates' *The Fun Starts Here*, to the autobiographical *Rape* by Jill Saward with Wendy Green.

There are also popular management titles (and management "stories"), books on food, film, politics and parenting. And their biography list is growing well.

Bloomsbury attracts a large number of unsolicited manuscripts and proposals: currently about 1,000 fiction manuscripts and 250 non-fiction proposals a year. The Bloomsbury editors are always looking for "quality and originality". Non-fiction proposals should comment as fully as possible on competitive titles. First-time writers are always advised to take great care over the presentation of their material.

Initial approach: fiction — a preliminary letter before sending anything, explaining briefly the type of novel it is. For non-fiction, the usual detailed synopsis, review of need, market and author's credentials, and two sample chapters.
Decisions: can take two months.
Terms: royalties and advances vary and are negotiable.

18

THE BODLEY HEAD LTD

Division of The Random Century
Group Ltd
Random Century House,
20 Vauxhall Bridge Road,
London SW1V 2SA

T: 071–973 9730

F: 8 (4)   . . .
[L, G, C, K]
NF: 20 (12)   . . .
[1, 2, 3]

Fiction and non-fiction: Jill Black or Charles Elliott
(Editorial Directors)

The Bodley Head celebrated its hundredth anniversary in 1987 — and
was taken over by Random House in the same year. It was founded by
John Lane; his nephew, Allen Lane, worked there for a while before
leaving to give birth to Penguin. The Bodley Head is now an imprint
within The Random Century Group.

In its early days, The Bodley Head published such top names as Aubrey
Beardsley and G. K. Chesterton, and launched the literary careers of
Agatha Christie and C. S. Forester. Since then it has attracted such
authors as Georgette Heyer, Graham Greene and Alastair Cooke. Current authors include Aleksandr Solzhenitzyn, Peter Dickinson and —
well known in writers' circles — Rhona Martin. Recent Bodley Head
fiction titles include Wayne Johnson's *The Snake Game* and Rudi van
Dantzig's *For a Lost Soldier*.

The non-fiction list is "up-market general" in character, with such
recent titles as Geoffrey Smith's *Reagan and Thatcher*, Nicholas Faith's
The World the Railways Made and Samuel Hynes's well-received *A War
Imagined*. There is also an illustrated, popular non-fiction list including
Mary Stewart-Wilson's *The Royal Mews* and *The Great Ormond Street
Book of Baby and Child Care*.

The Bodley Head children's list is now reported on as part of Random
Century Children's Books (*see* page 155).

Initial approach: fiction, preferably the first two chapters and a synopsis
of the rest; non-fiction — a detailed synopsis, an assessment of need and
market, the author's credentials, and — but not immediately — a couple
of sample chapters.
Decisions: usually within a couple of months, but sometimes take three.
Terms: royalties usually 10% of hardback and 7.5% of paperback list
price sales; advances can start at £1,500 for fiction and £2,000 for non-
fiction.

BUSINESS BOOKS

Div of The Random Century Group Ltd

F: NIL
NF: . . . (. .)   . . .
[6]

Random Century House
20 Vauxhall Bridge Road,
London SW1V 2SA

T: 071–973 9670

Non-fiction: Lucy Shankleman (Publishing Director)

Business Books (previously Hutchinson Business Books) is a separate imprint within The Random Century Group. As its name implies, it publishes exclusively non-fiction books; business books and books about management.

There are books on "soft management skills"; on communication techniques — I have a well-thumbed copy of Clive Goodworth's *Effective Speaking and Presentation* in my own bookshelves — and on negotiating (eg *Managing Negotiations* by Kennedy, Benson and McMillan); there are books on understanding accounts; there are books on a number of subjects by the prolific Greville Janner — recently, *Janner on Pitching for Business* — and there are books on different aspects of recruitment, such as Yvonne Sarch's recent *How to be Headhunted*. There are also books by major management gurus such as Richard J. Schonberger's *Building a Chain of Customers*. They also publish business "stories" — factual accounts of major business "turn-arounds", management achievements, etc.

In general, it could be said that Business Books are for the more senior business executive who is nearer to "making it" than are the more strictly "how to" books from other publishers. Business Books tend to assume a certain basic knowledge and experience.

Initial approach: Detailed chapter-by-chapter synopsis, assessment of the need for the book, and a statement of the author's credentials, plus a couple of sample chapters available for submission on request.
Decisions: Usually within a month.
Terms: The parent publisher is a signatory to the society of Authors/Writers' Guild Minimum Terms Agreement, which means royalties of 10% hb and 7.5% pb on list price for home sales — with good "royalty jumps".

CAMBRIDGE UNIVERSITY PRESS

Edinburgh Building, Shaftesbury Road,
Cambridge CB2 2RU

T: 0223 312393

```
F: NIL
NF: 1300 (1000)    10K
[1, 7, 8]
```

Non-fiction: The Specialist Editor (Subject name)

Founded in 1534, Cambridge University Press is rightly proud of its position as the world's oldest press. (On 20 July 1534, Henry VIII uniquely granted the Chancellor, Masters, and Scholars of the University of Cambridge "and their successors for ever", in Letters Patent, the "lawful and warranted power to print there all manner of books approved by the Chancellor or his deputy and three doctors . . . and also to exhibit for sale . . . wherever they please, all such books and all other books wherever printed.") The Press's backlist is immense — 10,000 titles.

The list is, of course, largely academic in nature. The titles are mostly under the "Humanities and Social Sciences" umbrella: arts, music, literature, religions, classical studies, philosophy, psychology, history, politics, economics and geography. Under "Sciences" come biology, chemistry, computer sciences, mathematics, medicine, physics and astronomy. There are also students' and children's educational books.

In the catalogue, amongst such "heavy" titles as — at random — R. M. W. Dixon's *The Dyirbal Language of North Queensland*, there are books which sound quite interesting to the lay reader. I was myself interested by the sound of Mattison Mines' *The Warrior Merchants: Textiles, Trade and Territory in South India*.

To write for Cambridge University Press you need to be a considerable expert, preferably in an academic field. But if you have the right knowledge and experience, CUP are very willing to consider proposals. About one in four proposals get accepted, and 75 per cent of writers are "first-timers".

The current list contains some interesting children's books — but these would need to have some educational "purpose" or link.

Initial approach: always, a written query first, to determine potential interest in your proposal; if interested, follow up with detailed synopsis, assessment of need and market, and author's credentials; thereafter, but not before, they may want a couple of sample chapters.
Decisions: can take several weeks.
Terms: royalties usually up to 10% of net receipts; advances are rare.

JONATHAN CAPE LTD

Div of The Random Century Group Ltd

F: 50 (10)	...
[L, C, S]	P
NF: 50 (15)	...
[1, 2, 3]	

Random Century House,
20 Vauxhall Bridge Road,
London SW1V 2SA

T: 071–973 9730

Fiction and non-fiction: Manuscript Submissions Department

One of the more prestigious of British publishers, Jonathan Cape was founded in 1921. Along with Chatto & Windus (*See* page 43) and Bodley Head (*See* page 29), they were taken over by the US publishers Random House in 1987. In 1989 Random House merged with Anthony Cheetham's Century Hutchinson to form the Random Century Group, of which Jonathan Cape is now a division.

Cape are a truly "general" publishing house with good strong fiction and non-fiction lists. In the past they have published such famous names as Ernest Hemingway, H. E. Bates, Irwin Shaw, and "Bond-man" Ian Fleming.

Today, their fiction authors are no less well-known. They include, among their recent titles: Philip Roth's *Deception*, Anita Brookner's *Brief Lives*, Kurt Vonnegut's *Hocus Pocus* and the string of new Bond books from the pen of John Gardner.

Cape's current non-fiction authors are no less prestigious than their novelists. Recent titles, in a very general list — hard to categorise — include Bernard Levin's *Now Read On*, Desmond Morris's *Animalwatching: A Field Guide to Animal Behaviour*, *A Complete Guide to British Moths* by Margaret Brooks, Eiko Ishioka's *Eiko by Eiko*, and top news photographer Don McCullin's *Unreasonable Behaviour: An Autobiography*.

They also publish poetry but only if the poet has already achieved some prior publication (in magazines, etc.); one recent title was Deborah Levy's 64-page paperback, *An Amorous Discourse in the Suburbs of Hell*. Submit poetry to Manuscript Submissions Department as for other work.

Cape's excellent children's list is now part of Random Century Children's Books — *see* page 155.

Initial approach: fiction — complete manuscripts preferred; non-fiction — the usual detailed synopsis, assessment of need, market and competition, author's credentials, and two sample chapters.
Decisions: one to three months.
Terms: royalties normally 10%/7.5% hb/pb on list price home sales; advances depend on assessment of potential.

CARCANET PRESS LTD

208 Corn Exchange
Manchester M4 3BQ

T: 061–834 8730

F: 7 (0)	100
[L]	P
Poetry: 24 (0)	130
NF: 12 (2)	80
[1]	

All (F, NF, poetry): Michael Schmidt (Editor)

Founded in 1969 but bought up in 1983 by its present owners, Carcanet is well-known as a major poetry publishing house. In recent years, however, it has also been expanding its literary fiction list. Overall, the Carcanet list comprises over 300 titles: 45% of the list is poetry, 25% biographies, memoirs and collected writings, and 30% fiction.

Much of the fiction list is made up of translations of European novels. Among the more prolific of the Carcanet authors are Italians Natalia Ginzburg, whose books include *Family* and *Valentino & Sagittarius*, and Leonardo Sciascia, who has written, notably, *Cronachette* and *The Council of Egypt*. There are also new novels from British writers Christine Brooke-Rose and Gabriel Josipovici (*The Big Glass*).

In the Lives and Letters sub-list there are collected columns by *Spectator* writer P. J. Kavanagh entitled *People and Places* and Malachi Whitaker's *And So Did I*.

But it is for its poetry that Carcanet is particularly renowned. Among the more recent titles are John Ash's latest collection, *The Burnt Pages* and Michael Hamburger's *Selected Poems*. Carcanet also publish many first collections of poems — recently by John Burnside and Sujata Bhatt, to name but two. They also revive the work of otherwise neglected poets of the past in their Fyfield Books imprint which has forty titles including the works of Oliver Goldsmith, Ben Jonson and Jonathan Swift.

Carcanet welcome new manuscripts in all parts of their list — "literary" fiction, lives and letters, and poetry. In an average year they receive something like 800 unsolicited manuscripts of all categories — of which they accept barely 5%. On the fiction side the odds are extremely long — they seldom take on more than one first novel a year.

Initial approach: for both fiction and non-fiction, a detailed synopsis plus two sample chapters is preferred. For poetry too, initially send samples only.
Decisions: usually within a month.
Terms: vary, and they are not prepared to specify.

CASSELL PLC

Villiers House, 41–47 Strand,
London WC2N 5JE

T: 071–839 4900

F: NIL
NF: 500 (200)   4000
[1–8 incl]

Non-fiction: Clare Howell, Editorial Director (General) *or* Stephen Butcher, Editorial Director (Academic & Educational)

Cassell PLC is an old-established publishing house (founded 1848) with several subsidiary imprints: Blandford, Arms and Armour, Geoffrey Chapman, Mansell, Mowbray, Studio Vista, and Ward Lock. Within those imprints Cassell covers the whole non-fiction field.

Blandford publish military history — as does Arms and Armour — natural history, craft and "New Age" books. Recent Blandford titles include *Medieval Warlords* by Tim Newark, *Grasshoppers and Mantids of the World* by Ken Preston-Mafham, *Ships in Bottles* by John Leopard, and *Celtic Gods and Goddesses* by Bob Stewart. They also publish *The Illustrated Guide to Bird Photography* by Bob Gibbons and Peter Wilson, and various other photographic books. Recent Arms and Armour books, all broadly *militaria*, include *The Napoleonic Source Book* by Philip J. Haythornthwaite, *Air War South Vietnam* by Robert F. Dorr, and *T-Class Submarines* by P. Kemp.

Cassell themselves are well-known for their dictionaries, and also, in the publishing world, for the annual *Directory of Publishing*. They also publish gardening books; recently for instance, Rob Proctor's *Antique Flowers: Perennials*, and the *Wisley Handbooks* series. Ward Lock titles deal mainly with cookery, gardening, and sports and hobbies. Recent titles include various *Mrs Beeton* books, *Small Gardens: A Creative Approach* by Page, Toogood, Baxendale and Courtier, and *Ahead of the Game: Squash* by David Pearson. Studio Vista concentrates on artistic topics; recent titles include *Scottish Painting 1837–1990* by William Hardie and *Japanese Quilts* by Jill Liddell and Yuko Watanabe.

The other Cassell imprints are more specialised. Geoffrey Chapman and Mowbray books are mainly religious/theological; Mansell books are largely academic, dealing with social and political topics. The Cassell imprint handles business and economics books and a large number of strictly educational books.

Initial approach: non-fiction only, synopsis plus market assessment and author's credentials, but initially without sample chapters.
Decisions: usually in one month but occasionally longer.
Terms: royalties normally, 7.5–10% hb, 5–7.5% pb on list price home sales. Advances vary with sales forecasts.

CENTURY BOOKS

Div of The Random Century Group Ltd

Random Century House,
20 Vauxhall Bridge Road,
London SW1V 2SA

T: 071–973 9750

```
F: 70 (. .)        . . .
[G, C, R, S]
NF: 110 (. .)      . . .
[1–5 incl]
```

Fiction and/or non-fiction: The Editorial Director

In 1985, Anthony Cheetham's dynamic Century publishing house took over the old-established (founded 1887) Hutchinson Publishing Group. Then, in 1989, Century Hutchinson joined Random House — parents of Jonathan Cape, The Bodley Head and Chatto & Windus — to form the new publishing giant, The Random Century Group.

Within Random Century, the individual imprints — as yet — still largely retain their own identities. Within this *Handbook* there are individual reports on: Hutchinson Books (including Frederick Muller (*see* page 97), Business Books (previously Hutchinson Business Books) (*see* page 31), The Bodley Head (see page 29), Jonathan Cape (see page 35), Chatto & Windus (*see* page 43), a grouped Random Century Children's Books (*see* page 155), and the paperback imprint Arrow Books (*see* page 17).

Century Books are generally slightly more "popular" than Hutchinson and the other imprints. Recent fiction titles include Joan Collins' *Love and Desire and Hate*, Maeve Binchy's *Circle of Friends*, and Fred Nolan's *Designated Assassin*. On the non-fiction side, recent Century titles such as Len Deighton's *Basic French Cookery*, *The Life and Death of Peter Sellers* by Roger Lewis, and Hugo Cornwall's *The Industrial Espionage Handbook* give a feel for the breadth of the list.

Century publish more specialised interest books under subsidiary imprints — "Legend" has such titles as *City of Truth*, a novella by James Morrow, while "Rider" caters for such non-fiction titles as *The Psychic Power of Children* by Cassandra Aason. And the imprint "Jill Norman Books" offers lavish books about food and drink.

Initial approach: Fiction — first three chapters and a synopsis; non-fiction: detailed synopsis, author's credentials, and assessment of market/need for the proposed book, with two sample chapters available to follow on request.

Decisions: Hopefully, within about a month.

Terms: Century Books are signatories to the Society of Authors/ Writers' Guild Minimum Terms Agreement — therefore royalties 10% hb, 7.5% pb on list price home sales — with good "royalty jumps".

CHATTO & WINDUS
(and THE HOGARTH PRESS)

Div of The Random Century Group Ltd

F: 50 (0)	345
[L,G, C, S, R]	P
NF: 35 (20)	340
[1, 2, 3, 4, 5]	

Random Century House,
20 Vauxhall Bridge Road,
London SW1V 2SA

T: 071–973 9740

Fiction and non-fiction: Jonathan Burnham (Editorial Director)
Poetry: Mick Imlah

Founded in 1855, Chatto & Windus took over Leonard and Virginia Woolf's The Hogarth Press in the 1940s; more recently, with Jonathan Cape (*see* page 35) and Bodley Head (*see* page 29) they have become part of The Random Century Group. However, Chatto/Hogarth remain a "quality" publisher, covering both fiction and general non-fiction — and poetry.

Chatto's current fiction list includes many top-line authors; Hogarth publishes a lot of re-issues. Recent Chatto fiction includes Erica Jong's *Any Woman's Blues*, Margaret Forster's *Lady's Maid*, Tariq Ali's *Redemption* and the *Complete Short Stories* of V. S. Pritchett. Recent Hogarth paperbacks include V. S. Pritchett's *Dublin*.

On the recent non-fiction side, Chatto include such titles as Jane Bown's *Portraits*, Iris Murdoch's *The Fire and the Sun*, the ubiquitous V. S. Pritchett's *Lasting Impressions*, and *The Man Between: A Biography of Carol Reed* by Nicholas Wapshott. Hogarth have *Freud on Women* edited by Elisabeth Young-Bruehl.

Chatto publish a small but ongoing amount of poetry. Recent titles have included *The Chatto Book of Love Poetry* and the *Collected Poems* of Norman MacCaig. Not long ago, they also published Fiona Pitt-Kethley's *Private Parts*.

Initial approach: Chatto & Windus will not consider unsolicited manuscripts — yet they receive up to 3,000 a year. They say they "simply do not have the time to read slush — it is returned by post (if sae enclosed) or destroyed. It is essential for new writers to approach publishers through agents." So . . . find yourself an agent; but note also that Chatto usually publish only one or two first novels a year. (The "0 out of 50" at the top of the page refers solely to 1990.)
Decisions: not applicable.
Terms: not applicable.

COLLINS CHILDREN'S BOOKS

Division of HarperCollins Publishers
77–85 Fulham Palace Road, London W6

T: 081–741 7070

F: 200 (1) [children's]	. . .
NF: 40 (20) [children's]	. . .

Fiction and non-fiction: Publishing Director, Children's Books

Collins Children's Books is a freestanding division within HarperCollins. Its list is comprehensive, covering everything from board picture books to reading for young teenagers.

There are the "Dinosaur" books — many by Althea, Michael Bond's Paddington Bear books, the many Enid Blyton books, and Alan Garner's lovely fantasies; and there are the *Little Grey Rabbit* books by Alison Uttley.

There are Armada Classics (in paperback) of such titles as *Wind in the Willows* by Kenneth Grahame and *Little Women* by Louisa M. Alcott. There are books by top science-fiction writer Harry Harrison (*The California Iceberg*), by Rosemary Friedman (*Aristide*) and by Richard Severy (*Burners and Breakers*).

There are Lions and Young Lions (both paperback imprints) with such titles as *Dragon Days*, *The Last Vampire*, and *The Inflatable Shop* — all by Willis Hall, *My Best Fiend* (no, that's not a misprint) by Sheila Lavelle, *The Demon Bike Rider* by Robert Leeson and, recently, *Spellhorn* by Berlie Doherty.

In the even younger Picture Lions picturebook imprint, recent titles have included *This Old Car* by Colin and Jacqui Hawkins and *Little Bunnie's Noisy Friends* by Harriet Zeifert.

Collins Children's Division has something for all age-groups, all formats, all prices.

Initial approach: fiction — the complete manuscript; non-fiction — send a brief query first, outlining the scope of the proposed book.
Decisions: can take six weeks.
Terms: not disclosed.

COLLINS GENERAL DIVISION

(including Collins Harvill)
Division of HarperCollins Publishers
77–85 Fulham Palace Road, London W6

T: 081–741 7070

F: 120 (20) . . .
[L, G, C, S, R]
NF: 70 (50) . . .
[1–4 incl, 6] H

Fiction and non-fiction: The New Manuscripts Editor

COLLINS REFERENCE DIVISION

(Incl: Collins Willow, leisure books and specific reference books)

F: NIL
NF: 200 (30) . . .
[2–5 incl, 8]

Non-fiction: Robin Wood (Publishing Director)

William Collins, Sons & Co Ltd — as, until recently, it was known — was one of the oldest British publishing houses, founded in 1819. In 1989, it was purchased by Rupert Murdoch's News International Group. It now forms the UK base of HarperCollins Publishers which incorporates the earlier Collins divisions and imprints — General Division, Children's Division (*see* page 45), Collins Harvill, Fontana (see page 67), Grafton Books (*see* page 79), etc., — plus the more recent acquisitions — Thorsons (*see* page 181) and Unwin Hyman.

Collins General Division publishes both fiction and non-fiction, in hardback. (Fontana is the paperback associate of Collins General Division.) Among recent Collins fiction titles have been best-seller Sidney Sheldon's *Memories of Midnight*, Susan Howatch's *Scandalous Risks*, Fay Weldon's *Darcy's Utopia*, and William Horwood's *Duncton Tales*. There is also the 1989 Woman of the Year, Aileen Armitage's latest, *Chapter of Shadows* and Maisie Mosco's *For Love and Duty*. And J. G. Ballard, previously with Grafton, has a recent Collins title, *War Fever*.

Within the General Division there is also the famous Crime Club series. Here, recent titles have included, to pick at random, *One Small Step* by the prolific Reginald Hill, *Gamelord* by Roger Parkes, and *Judge and be Damned* by Janet Edmonds. There are four new Crime Club books published each month. The market is large.

On the non-fiction side, the General Division has recently published such titles as *The Ark's Anniversary* by Gerald Durrell, a biography, *Stanley Spencer* by Ken Pople, *Winston Churchill: His Life as a Painter* by his daughter, Mary Soames, the official biography of *King Edward VIII* by Philip Zeigler, and . . . *The Collins Book of Love Poems*.

The Collins Harvill imprint — mainly up-market non-fiction, but some fiction too — has recently published *De Gaulle: The Rebel: 1890–1944*

28

by Jean Lacouture and *The Russian Revolution* by Richard Pipes. (Both sell at £25 each!) In fiction, Harvill have recently published *The Keeper of Antiquities* by Yury Dombrovsky and *The Marquis of Bolibar* by Leo Perutz. But they also published the less "heavy" G. MacDonald Fraser's latest, *Flashman and the Mountain of Light*.

Collins Reference Division (including not only reference books "proper", but also books on various leisure interests and the specifically sports-oriented Collins Willow Books) publishes exclusively non-fiction. Recent non-reference titles have included *Basingstoke Boy* by John Arlott (in Willow), *The Trials of Life* by David Attenborough and Alan Toogood's *Collins Garden Trees Handbook*. On the reference side there are such recent titles as Ian Chambers' *Gem Basic Facts: Business Studies* and Eric Deeson's *Collins Dictionary of Information Technology*.

Initial approach: fiction — General Division (and Fontana, who share a common editorial staff) prefer to see the first two chapters and a synopsis of the rest of the novel. They receive about 4000 unsolicited manuscripts each year so, understandably, they emphasise yet again the need for return postage and for work to be typed.

Non-fiction — General Division (with Fontana again sharing editorial staff) prefer to see a detailed synopsis, an assessment of need and market, the author's credentials, and two sample chapters. The Reference Division prefers a written query first, outlining the broad scope and content of the proposed book.

Decisions: usually within a month — but Reference Division sometimes up to three months.

Terms: HarperCollins will not disclose terms.

CONSTABLE & CO. LTD

3 The Lanchesters,
162 Fulham Palace Road,
London W6 9ER

T: 081-741 3663

F: 30 (10)   200
[L, C]
NF: 40 (12)   500
[1, 2, 3]

Fiction: Robin Baird-Smith (Editorial Director) or Candida Brazil. Miles Huddleston (Thrillers)
Non-fiction: Benjamin Glazebrook (Chairman), Robin Baird-Smith or Candida Brazil

Constable Publishers was founded in 1890 — it has just celebrated its centenary. The company remains independent, and has a list of several hundred books.

The Constable catalogue divides roughly into 25% fiction, 75% non-fiction. The fiction list is split roughly 50/50 between "literary" and crime/suspense genre titles. The non-fiction list is particualrly strong in biographies.

Constables have published some really big names — from Walter Scott to George Bernard Shaw, Katherine Mansfield to Bram Stoker and Dos Passos to Damon Runyon. Today's fiction list maintains this tradition with, for example, Muriel Spark's *Symposium* and Anita Mason's *The Racket*.

Recent additions to the ever-lively Constable Crime list include *Funnelweb* by Russell Braddon, *The Seven Sleepers* by Elizabeth Ferrars, and *Daphne Dead and Done For* by Jonathan Ross.

On the non-fiction side too, the standards are well maintained with such as *Howard Carter*, H. V. F. Winstone's biography of the discoverer of Tutankhamun's tomb, and John Julius Norwich's *Venice: A Traveller's Companion*. At a lighter level, there is the *Geordie Scrapbook* by Joe Ging and Brian Redhead, and broadcaster Brian Matthew's autobiography.

Novelists in the North of England are reminded of the annual Constable Trophy for a previously unpublished novel, which offers a £1,000 prize, a silver cup, and consideration for publication by Constables (with an advance of a further £1,000). Details from The Literature Dept., Northern Arts, 10 Osborne Terrace, Newcastle upon Tyne NE2 1NZ.

Initial approach: fiction — write first and then send the first few chapters and a synopsis. Non-fiction — letter with detailed synopsis, assessment of need, and author's credentials — sample chapters ready to follow.
Decisions: can take up to three months.
Terms: royalties of 10% hb and 7.5% pb on list price, with a "royalty jump" when hardback sales exceed 2500. Advances not less than £1,500 for a novel or £2,000 for a non-fiction book.

CORGI BOOKS
(and all other Transworld pb imprints,
see below)

F: 120 (25) [all]	1150
NF: 20 (10) [1–6 incl]	250
	H

Division of Transworld Publishers Ltd
61–63 Uxbridge Road, London W5 5SA

T: 081–579 2652/9

Corgi & Black Swan, F & NF: Patrick Janson-Smith (Pub. Dir.)
Bantam (pb) F & NF: Anthony Mott (Pub. Dir.)
All Children's hb/pb, F/NF: Philippa Dickinson (Publishing Director)

Transworld Publishers, of which Corgi is the main paperback imprint —
with Bantam chasing hard — were founded in 1950. Overall Transworld
publish Corgi, Black Swan, Bantam, Young Corgi, Yearling and Bantam
Computer Books in paperback. Their hardback imprints, led by Bantam
Press (*see* page 19), include Bantam Press, Doubleday, Partridge Press,
and Doubleday Children's Books.

The paperback imprints are basically reprint publishers; they are all
grouped together on this page. Similarly, all Transworld children's books
including the hardback Doubleday Children's Books are commented on
here.

Both Corgi and Bantam are mass-market imprints with many titles in
both "general popular" fiction and the various *genres*. Leading Corgi
authors include Catherine Cookson, Jilly Cooper, Frederick Forsyth,
Danielle Steel and Anne McCaffrey to name but a few. Leading Bantam
authors include Judith Krantz, Charlotte Bingham, Elizabeth George and
Tim Sebastian.

Black Swan is a more literary imprint; their authors include Mary
Wesley, John Irving and Stan Barstow.

Across the paperback lists, the non-fiction titles include many biographies, a range of management books, a lot of health, diet, "New Age"
and psychology books — and a shelf-full of humour books.

Transworld Children's range from Picture Corgis (eg Frank Muir's
What-a-Mess books) through Young Corgis (5–9) such as *Dragon Fire*
and *Dragon Earth* by Ann Ruffell, to the Yearling (8–11) series. The
Yearling series includes such recent titles as Dave Morris's *Teenage
Mutant Hero Turtles* books, Robert Swindells' 1990 Children's Book
Award winner *Room 13* and Tony Bradman's *Sam, The Girl Detective*
books. Recent titles in the Doubleday Children's hardback imprint
include Robert Swindells' *Dracula's Castle* and Dick King-Smith's *Jungle
Jingles*. For "young adult" readers, Bantam offer a huge range of
stories — mainly US imports.

Initial approach: preferably through an agent; if not, always a preliminary letter.

Decisions: can take up to three months.

Terms: pb royalties 7.5% (and up) on list price home sales. Advances vary — from £1,500 upwards.

DAVID & CHARLES PUBLISHERS PLC

(Part of The Reader's Digest Group)
Brunel House, Newton Abbot,
Devon TQ12 4PU

T: 0626 61121

F: NIL	NIL
NF: 75 (20) [2, 3, 4, 5]	250

Non-fiction: Piers Spence (Editorial Director)

Founded in 1960 by two transport enthusiasts, David St John Thomas (railway buff) and Charles Hadfield (canal fan), David & Charles is now part of The Reader's Digest Group. David & Charles has long been renowned for the quality of its book production; and it has always been strong in books about railways and canals.

Today, David & Charles have spread their interests wider: the current list is also strong in craft and hobby books, in books about the countryside and country and nature interests, and in practical "how-to-do-it" books. They are popular with "country" type writers — and others — and receive about 750 non-fiction book proposals each year; they publish a tenth of that amount. But they have not broadened their interests as wide as the optimism of some budding authors: strictly non-fiction publishers, they still receive around 200 unsolicited novels a year.

With the acquisition of the company in July 1990 by Reader's Digest, the list is likely to reduce in size and the books themselves to become bigger and more colourful.

Typical of the current titles in their list are *The Mighty Rainforest* by John Nichol; Graham Downing's *The Fields in Winter*; *Cross Stitch Cards and Keepsakes* by best-selling crafts author, Jo Verso; *The Great Anglers* by John Bailey; and *The Book of Primroses* by botanical artist Barbara Shaw.

(David & Charles also own the Readers' Union Book Clubs — leaders in their field.)

Initial approach: they prefer just a written query briefly outlining the subject of the proposed non-fiction book.
Decisions: can take up to three months.
Terms: they pay royalties of 15% of net receipts on hardback sales and 10% of net receipts on paperback sales; they decline to quote a likely figure for advances, but advise that for the right books, they can be substantial.

J. M. DENT & SONS LTD

Subsidiary of George Weidenfeld &
Nicolson (Holdings) Ltd
Clapham High Street,
London SW4 7TA

T: 071–622 9933

F: 30 (6) . . .
[children's only]
NF*: 20 (3) . .   91
[1–5 incl, 7]
* adults only

Non-fiction: Malcolm Gerratt (Editorial Director)
Children's fiction: Fiona Kennedy (Children's Publisher)

Founded in 1888, J. M. Dent are of course well known for their Everyman's Library series, at least one book from which must surely grace the shelves in most homes. (I would be lost without my Everyman's *Dictionary of Quotations and Proverbs* and my *Encyclopaedia*.) They are now part of the equally prestigious, but younger, George Weidenfeld & Nicolson Ltd. They are expanding their Everyman paperback list.

Apart from the Everyman's Library, their backlist is graced by such names as Dylan Thomas and Joseph Conrad. The emphasis is now on authoritative non-fiction, with "good backlist potential" in — specifically — reference, music, gardening and some biography. Typical recent titles include *The Dent Dictionary of Fictional Characters* by Martin Seymour-Smith, *Companion to Baroque Music* edited by Julie Anne Sadie and *W. B. Yeats: The Poems* edited by Daniel Albright.

The Dent children's list is alive and thriving; it is now concentrating on picture books and fiction up to teenage level. Recent picture book titles include *Michael's Monster* by Pamela Gandham, *Santa's Sneeze* by David Ross, and *Nicholas and the Rocking-horse* by Jean Richardson. For slightly older readers, aged 6+, there is *Pig* by Alan Gibbons and *Mallory Cox and his Magic Socks* by Andrew Matthews.

Initial approach: no general adult fiction or poetry at all; non-fiction only — detailed synopsis, assessment of need and market and author's credentials (have sample chapters ready). Children's fiction: synopsis and two sample chapters.
Decisions: can take up to two months.
Terms: "variable".

ANDRÉ DEUTSCH LTD

105–106 Great Russell Street,
London WC1B 3LJ

T: 071–580 2746

F: 80 (24)	**840**
[L, G, C, R, K]	
NF: 40 (30)	**420**
[1, 2, 3, 4, 5]	**H**

Adult Fiction: Esther Whitby (Editorial Director)
Children's fiction: Pamela Royds (Children's Editorial Director)

André Deutsch was founded in 1950. Since then, it has built up a sizeable reputation and a large, quality, backlist. They are good on general fiction and non-fiction and have a good children's list too.

Among the top authors in their backlist are V. S. Naipaul, George Mikes (the professional alien), Peter Benchley, Penelope Lively, and cider-man Laurie Lee. Recent fiction titles are well up to the same high standards; they include Carlos Fuentes' *Constancia and Other Stories for Virgins*, *Those in Peril* by Nicolas Freeling, Gore Vidal's *Hollywood*, and *Ripley Bogle* by Robert Wilson. And there is always John Updike — with his numerous *Rabbit* books.

The new non-fiction list too has many major titles. Recent titles include Phillip Knightley's *Philby: KGB Masterspy*, Jill Cox and Tony Lord's *Which Food, Which Wine*, and Elias Canetti's *The Play of the Eyes*.

The children's book list is equally good. At the picture book end, where they are particularly strong, there are all John Cunliffe's *Postman Pat* books — and his new *Big Jim, Little Jim*. There are also such recent picture book titles as Edwina Eddy's *Enoch the Hungry* and Rebecca Vickers' *Head Lice from Outer Space* (No, that's not a misprint! I'm tempted to buy it).

For the middle years, there are books by Michael Rosen and Penelope Lively to name but two. Deutsch also have a teenage imprint, their ADLIB paperbacks. Recent titles here include *Someone Else's Baby* by Geraldine Kaye, *The Highest Form of Killing* by Malcolm Rose and Denis Hamley's *Coded Signals*.

André Deutsch are offered a huge number of unsolicited manuscripts, about 2,500 novels and 1,000 non-fiction book ideas each year. They welcome this, and consider them all carefully; the number of new novels and new non-fiction writers they actually accept however is proportionally *very* small.

Initial approach: fiction — first chapter only, and **no** synopsis; for non-fiction, they prefer just a written query, briefly outlining subject and coverage.
Decisions: usually within one month.
Terms: they prefer not to specify.

EBURY PRESS

Div of The Random Century Group Ltd

F: NIL
NF: 60 (15)   . . .
[1, 2, 3, 4]

Random Century House,
20 Vauxhall Bridge Road,
London SW1V 2SA

T: 071–973 9690

Non-fiction: Fiona McIntyre (Editorial Director)

A high quality non-fiction publisher, Ebury Press was founded in the 1960s as the book-publishing imprint of the National Magazine Company (*Good Housekeeping, SHE, Cosmopolitan*, etc.). During 1989 it was bought by Century Hutchinson; it is now part of The Random Century Group.

Its present stocklist contains several hundred titles; it is inevitably strong on home interest subjects — cookery, arts and crafts, family and health — which take up more than half the list. There are also popular biographies, with travel, photography and guide books making up about a quarter of the list.

Part of the list is exclusively filled with *Good Housekeeping* books and books linked to other National Magazine titles. There are one-off titles too, covering a broad range of subjects from health, and nostalgia, to self-help. Within the home interest area there are several series; the "Pocket Guides" Series (*Crochet, Knitting, Needlework*), "The Harrods Collection" (*Harrods Book of Entertaining, Harrods Wedding Book*, etc.), and "The Ritz Collection" (*Ritz Book of Afternoon Tea, . . . of Christmas*).

Among recent Ebury titles are *The Good Housekeeping Freezer to Microwave Encyclopaedia, Decorative Victorian Needlework* by Elizabeth Bradley, *The 1991 Good Pub Guide* edited by Alisdair Aird, *Sultans of Style* by Georgina Howell, and *Last of the Hot Metal Men* by Derek Jamieson. Very varied but all very much "in an Ebury mould".

Initial approach: requiring non-fiction only, they prefer the usual detailed synopsis, assessment of the need for the book, the likely market and the competition, author's credentials, and a couple of sample chapters.
Decisions: can take up to three months.
Terms: Ebury will not specify royalty rates, etc.

ELEMENT BOOKS

The Old Schoolhouse, The Courtyard,
Bell Street, Shaftesbury,
Dorset SP7 8BP

T: 0747 51448

F: NIL
NF: 80 (50)
...
[1, philosophy, ancient wisdom, health etc.]

Non-fiction: The Editorial Director

Element Books specialise in publishing somewhat esoteric books which, without themselves changing, seem to be becoming less esoteric as the world "catches up".

Their main series, and the one for which they most welcome ideas/submissions is *The Elements of* . . . series. Typical recent titles range from *The Elements of Dreamwork* by Strephon Kaplan-Williams, . . . *of Christian Symbolism* by John Baldock, . . . *of Sufism* by Shaykh Fadhlalla Haeri, and . . . *of Herbalism* by David Hoffmann. All the books in this series are well-illustrated paperbacks; they seem to publish four new *Elements of* . . . books each quarter. New writers would be well advised to study (any) one of the books in the series very carefully, before submitting a proposal — there is a series "image".

Other recent titles — "one-offs", not in *The Elements of* . .. series — include *The Body-Mind Workbook* by Debbie Shapiro, *Colin Wilson: The Man and his Mind* by Howard Dossor, and *Dreamlife: Understanding and Using Your Dreams* by David Fontana.

These titles give a good "feel" for the somewhat unusual types of books published — and eagerly sought — by Element Books. Non-fiction books should be a minimum of 30,000 words in length, but some books can be acceptable up to about 100,000 words.

They say, "A clear idea, with a *real* market in mind can quickly engage the publisher's interest. A well-presented synopsis and sample chapters in an attractive binder will encourage the publisher to take the author more seriously." And, flippantly (I think), "Anything that can be read in the bath, without all the pages falling into the water, might well result in a contract!"

A purely non-fiction publisher, Element are offered around 200 novels per year. (So much for writers' market research.) Somewhat more realistically, they receive about 3,000 non-fiction books or synopses a year too. For an annual output of around 80 the competition is fierce.

Initial approach: synopsis, assessment of need and market, author's credentials, and two sample chapters.
Decisions: usually within one month.
Terms: royalties of 10% of hb/trade-pb list price for home sales; 10% of net receipts on overseas sales; advances £500 and upwards.

ELLIOT RIGHT WAY BOOKS

Kingswood Buildings,
Lower Kingswood,
Tadworth, Surrey KT20 6TD

T: 0737 832202

F: NIL	NIL
NF: 15 (11)	150
[3, 4, 5, 6]	H

Non-fiction: Malcolm Elliot (Director)

Founded in 1948, Elliot Right Way Books is a strictly non-fiction publisher. Interestingly, they still receive about a hundred, wholly inappropriate, unsolicited fiction manuscripts per year — emphasising the need for market research (and a book such as this). The firm's name derives from the original titles, which were all *The Right Way to . . .*; their current books too are all very much in the "How to" mould, but with less restrictive titles. Many of their current books are published in their inexpensive "Paperfronts" series.

There are Paperfronts "how to" books on a wide variety of crafts, hobbies, sports and general management topics. Among listed titles are *The Right Way to Apply for a Job* (interestingly, reverting to the original imprint approach), *Sample Social Speeches*, and *Micro-Computers for Business & Home*. Other titles deal with aspects of cooking, health, petcare, DIY, etc. Recent titles include *Buying a Used Car* by Kenneth Salmon and *The After Work Cook* by Maggic Brogan — all very practical and useful.

They say, "We are rigorously selective in the choice of books we publish. We set the highest standards of editorial quality and accuracy." Their selective approach means that they can achieve large print runs, low prices — and a mass market.

They are always interested in hearing from those expert in some field who think there might be a book in it. Elliots offer help to such inexperienced authors; but, of course, are happier with a more professional approach. They receive, on average, over 250 new non-fiction book submissions per year; less than 10 per cent are accepted — but 90% of these are by new Elliot writers. They prefer new non-fiction books to be between 35,000 and 60,000 words in length.

Initial approach: preferably, a detailed synopsis, a written appreciation of the need and market for the book, the author's credentials, and a couple of sample chapters. But remember, they will help inexperienced writers who are expert in their field.
Decisions: usually within a month.
Terms: an unspecified but "generous" percentage on every copy sold in all markets (with advances "up to £500"), *or* outright purchase of copyright (author's choice).

FABER & FABER LTD

3 Queen Square, London WC1N 3AU

T: 071–278 6881

F: 60 (10)	. . .
[L, G, C, K]	P
NF: 200 (60)	. . .
[1, 2, 3, 4]	H

Fiction and non-fiction: The Editorial Department
Poetry: The Poetry Editor

A prestigious publishing house with a high-quality list extending also to much fine poetry and drama, Faber & Faber was founded in the 1920s. Past authors include T. S. Eliot, Ezra Pound, Philip Larkin, Sylvia Plath and James Joyce. Current writers include P. D. James, Samuel Beckett, Tom Stoppard and Milan Kundera.

Recent hardback fiction titles include *The Dwarfs* by Harold Pinter, *The Clopton Hercules* by Duncan Sprott and *Great Climate* by Michael Wilding. All high quality. Titles published in paperback include *Laughable Loves* by Milan Kundera, *We Are Still Married* by Garrison Keillor, and *The Fat Man in History* by Peter Carey.

The non-fiction list is diverse and distinguished too. Recent titles include *Caesar's Vast Ghost: Aspects of Provence* by Lawrence Durrell, *The Palace of Varieties* by Julian Critchley, *Wine Snobbery: An Insider's Guide to the Booze Business* by Andrew Barr, and *Scorsese on Scorsese* edited by David Thompson and Ian Christie.

Recent poetry titles include Philip Larkin's *Collected Poems* and *The Faber Book of Blue Verse* edited by John Whitworth. On the drama side, recent publications include *Tom Stoppard: The Radio Plays 1964–1983*, *Redevelopment: Slum Clearance* by Vaclav Havel and *Invisible Friends* by Alan Ayckbourn.

The Faber children's list is of similar quality to the adult list. Recent fiction, non-fiction and poetry titles include *Inside the Glasshouse* by Giles Diggle, *Calico the Wonder Horse* by Virginia Lee Burton, *Composer's World: Mozart* by Wendy Thompson, and *Dragonfire and Other Poems* by Judith Nicholls.

Faber say that they are always interested in seeing work from new writers and promise that everything is carefully read; but their standards are very high. They also make a strong plea for the provision of an adequately sized stamped self-addressed envelope.

Initial approach: fiction — the full manuscript; non-fiction — detailed synopsis, assessment, author's credentials and two sample chapters.
Decisions: usually within a month.
Terms: royalties 10% hb, 7.5% pb on list price home sales, with good "royalty jumps". Advances vary.

FONTANA PAPERBACKS

Division of HarperCollins Publishers
77–85 Fulham Palace Road, London W6

T: 081–741 7070

F: 130 (20)	. . .
[L, G, C, S, R]	
NF: 80 (60)	. . .
[1, 2, 3, 6]	H

Fiction and non-fiction: The New Manuscripts Editor

Fontana is the paperback associate of Collins General Division, within HarperCollins; it is to some extent in competition with Grafton paperbacks (*see* page 79). As a reprint house, and as would be expected, Fontana Paperbacks have a very similar list to that of Collins General Division — but they do reprint other publishers books too.

The Fontana fiction list includes such authors as Craig Thomas, Sydney Sheldon, Hammond Innes, Tom Clancy, Susan Howatch, Winston Graham, Julia Fitzgerald, Alistair MacNeill and Victoria Holt. Recent books include, from Martin Cruz Smith, the author of *Gorky Park*, *Polar Star*, from Patrick O'Brian *The Thirteen-Gun Salute*, and from the late — much-missed — Julia Fitzgerald, *Earth Queen, Sky King*. On the fantasy front, a recent Anthony Swithin title — starting a new series — was *Princes of Sandastre*.

On the non-fiction side, Fontana are strong on management techniques, politics and contemporary affairs. In common with other reprint houses, Fontana publish some new non-fiction titles of their own initiation. They welcome *relevant* proposals.

Initial approach: for both fiction and non-fiction, Fontana share editorial staff with Collins General Division (*see* page 46) and submissions should therefore be sent to The New Manuscripts Editor there — always typed, and always accompanied by adequate return postage.

For fiction they prefer to see the first two chapters and a synopsis of the rest; for non-fiction a detailed synopsis, an assessment of need and market, the author's credentials, and two sample chapters.
Decisions: usually within a month.
Terms: HarperCollins will not disclose terms.

W. FOULSHAM & CO LTD

Yeovil Road, Slough, Berks SL1 4JH

T: 0753 26769

F: NIL
NF: 55 (30)   250
[2–8 incl]

Non-fiction: Foulsham — The Controlling Editor
Quantum — Bill Anderton

Founded in 1819, one of Foulsham's greatest claims to fame is, of course, the annual *Old Moore's Almanack*. But Foulsham publish much more than just *Old Moore*: in their backlist they have reference books, books on wine, food, cookery and health, craft and DIY books, a whole series of books on the martial arts, books on sports and on petcare, books on the occult and a range of technical and educational books. Their list is wholly non-fiction and, generally, very practical.

They have recently launched a slightly less practical list; their new "New Age" imprint Quantum, is "dedicated to the realisation of human potential and its practical applications". Typical Quantum titles include Les Peto's *The Dream Lover* and Editor Bill Anderton's own *Life Cycles: The Astrology of Inner Space*. If you are a "New Age" writer, try Quantum.

The mainstream Foulsham imprint is more practical. Recent titles include E. L. Mayoh's *Win That Job*, *Direct Your Subconscious and Drive to Success* by Paul Harris, *The Best Wine Buys in the High Street* by Judy Ridgeway, and *Make Your Home Video More Professional* by David Owen (a BBC TV man). And some management/self-help books by myself are in the pipeline.

Foulsham also publish more general non-fiction books. Recent general-interest titles include *Bob Hope: Thanks for the Memory* by Peter Haining and *Atlantic Jeopardy* (modern naval history) by Paul Lund and Harry Ludlam.

Foulsham publish a useful selection of books for teachers. One series is called "Lessons at a Moment's Notice"; subjects include religious education, maths, science, art and remedial studies. They also publish a best-selling *101 School Assembly Stories* — every secondary school needs one.

Initial approach: Foulsham prefer a written query before a manuscript is submitted; send them a brief assessment of the need/market for the book, a statement of your credentials, and a detailed synopsis.
Decisions: may take three months.
Terms: normally 10% of net receipts (worth about 6% of list price); advances vary widely — from zero up.

FOURTH ESTATE LTD

289 Westbourne Grove,
London W11 2QA

T: 071–727 8993

F: 15 (5)	26
[L, G]	
NF: 15 (5)	56
[1–5 incl]	H

Fiction: Giles O'Bryen (Commissioning Editor)
Non-fiction: Christopher Potter (Commissioning Editor)

Fourth Estate is a small publisher holding its own in a world of faceless conglomerates; it was founded in 1984 and won the *Sunday Times* small publishers award in 1988. And the firm's young directors are working hard at growing bigger — they plan to double their annual output (currently 30-plus books per year) in the next year or so.

Among the better-known authors with titles appearing in Fourth Estate's list are Auberon Waugh, Jeffrey Bernard (a book about horses) and Karen Blixen. They are particularly proud of their discovery of Adam Zameenzad — who won the 1987 David Higham Prize for Best First Novel with his *The Thirteenth House*. They have recently published his fourth novel, *Cyrus Cyrus*.

On the non-fiction side, recent titles include a biography of rock star Jimi Hendrix, *Are You Experienced?* by Noel Redding and Carol Appleby, *This Literary Life*, a book of cartoons about the literary world by Peter van Straaten, and *Back Where I Came From* — about New York in its heyday of speakeasies and markets — by A. J. Leibling.

Fourth Estate have recently introduced a new imprint — Guardian Books. Apart from the latest edition of the long established *Bedside Guardian* and a collection of ten years of Guardian Film Lectures *Talking Films*, the new imprint also includes 60 linked episodes of the delightful *Dulcie Domum's Bad Housekeeping* "diary", now known to be from the pen of Sue Limb. (They are always the first thing I turn to in the *Weekend Guardian*.) They also have a Blueprint Monographs imprint — for books on design and architecture.

Fourth Estate say that they are always on the lookout for bold, unusual, distinctive writers. They are concerned that abroad, the English novel is now regarded as small and insular — and are looking for writing that will reverse that view.

Initial approach: for both fiction and non-fiction, they prefer a synopsis and two sample chapters.
Decisions: can take up to three months.
Terms: "industry standard" royalties of 10% hardback, 7.5% paperback on list prices for home sales. Advances range from £1000 for a first novel to, they say, £50,000 for established authors.

SAMUEL FRENCH LTD

52 Fitzroy Street, London W1P 6JR

T: 071–387 9373

<table>
<tr><td colspan="2">Plays: 60 (5)   1500
[Crime, Comedy,
Straight, Panto,
Children's]</td></tr>
</table>

All play scripts to: Play Submissions Department

Samuel French Ltd is a long-established publisher of plays — they were founded in 1830. Their list contains approximately 1,500 titles in print, primarily intended for performance by amateur drama companies.

In an average year they will receive 250–300 unsolicited play manuscripts; few will previously have been professionally produced. Among the most well-known playwrights who are published by Samuel French are Noel Coward and Alan Ayckbourn. But many French plays have not had the benefit of a major London performance; they publish four or five plays by previously unpublished writers each year. About three-quarters of their plays are "full-length" only a quarter are one-act plays.

They advise new writers: "Thrillers and comedies are easier to place with dramatic societies than are straight dramas, which frequently need the publicity generated by major, preferably West End, productions in order to make them attractive publishing propositions. The ordinary amateur group avoids plays with contentious subject matter. The same rulings apply with respect to the use of expletives and "bad" language. Size of cast is no obstacle to amateur companies, provided that the *dramatis personae* does not stretch to 30-odd characters. However, amateur groups traditionally have more female members than male ones and consequently a play with a majority of male acting roles is more difficult to sell than is a script that has a lot of good women's parts.

"Other popular *genres* are pantomimes and children's plays. However, the competition in this area is extremely fierce; pantomime writing is far more difficult than one might imagine. Many schoolteachers submit the plays which they have written for their school, and this market is therefore somewhat oversubscribed.

"At the same time, the demands of school drama societies are changing rapidly, and the growing youth theatre movement has created a demand for plays of especial relevance to teenagers' experience. We are therefore eager to find good, well-written texts which will appeal to these new markets."

Initial approach: submit synopsis, cast and setting requirements, and specimen scene; not the full manuscript.
Decisions: can take three months plus.
Terms: Samuel French will not divulge details.

FUTURA BOOKS

A division of Macdonald & Co Ltd
Orbit House, 1 New Fetter Lane,
London EC4A 1AR

T: 071–377 4600

F: 110 (15)	800
[L, G, C, S, R, W]	
NF: 40 (20)	300
[1, 2, 3, 4]	H

Fiction and non-fiction: Editorial Department (Macdonald–Futura)

One of the paperback imprints of Macdonald & Co (*see* page 109), many (but not all) Futura paperback titles are acquired jointly with the Macdonald hardcover. Macdonald Futura is a vertically integrated editorial division. From agents and other publishers, they receive something like 3,000 unsolicited manuscripts each year.

Among well-known Futura titles — many also included in the Macdonald list — are Iain Banks' *The Wasp Factory*, Colleen McCullough's *The Thorn Birds* and Larry Niven's *Neutron Star*. There are also the *Brother Cadfael* mysteries of Ellis Peters and the many Catherine Cookson novels. Recent fiction releases include Beryl Kingston's *Sixpenny Stalls*, Jonathan Kellerman's *Silent Partner* and Sarah Harrison's *Cold Feet* (the sequel to her earlier, hilarious, *Hot Breath*).

On the non-fiction side, Catherine Cookson's recent autobiography *Our Kate* is noteworthy. Futura also publish a lot of true crime books, such as Joe McGinniss's *Blind Faith*. They have also published Maureen Lipman's delightfully humorous books — *How Was It For You?* and *Something to Fall Back On* — and Gary Larson's cult *Far Side* cartoon books.

Initial approach: fiction — like most mass-market paperback publishers, Futura are essentially a reprint house. They do not welcome the manuscripts of unpublished novels — which should be processed through Macdonald. On the non-fiction side however, they do publish some original material, for which they require the usual synopsis, assessment of need and market, author's credentials and two sample chapters.
Decisions: can take three months.
Terms: in common with other Macdonald divisions, Futura do not disclose terms — but royalties are seldom less than "the standard" (7.5% for paperback).

VICTOR GOLLANCZ LTD

Subsidiary of Houghton Mifflin Co. USA

14 Henrietta Street, London WC2E 8QJ

T: 071–836 2006

F: 167 (7)	590
[L, G, K, C, S]	
NF: 66 (16)	660
[1, 2, 3, 4, 5, 7]	

Fiction and non-fiction: The Editor . . . (General fiction, SF, Crime, Non-fiction, Children's, etc. as appropriate.)

The Victor Gollancz publishing house was founded by . . . Victor Gollancz in 1928. It was bought by the American publisher Houghton Mifflin Co. of Boston in 1989. Before the War, Gollancz was renowned for its Left Book Club books (some still on my shelves) and for its yellow-jacketed crime books; to this day it remains a notable house of "good reads" and particularly strong on crime and science fiction.

They are offered something like 2,600 new novels a year in all categories: they publish less than 7% of that number — and only a handful (7 in 1990) are first novels. (You are most likely to succeed, here or with any other publisher, with a genre novel.)

The Gollancz backlist is full of famous names: they have published the novels of A. J. Cronin, of Dorothy L. Sayers and of Daphne du Maurier. Current general fiction titles include *Stripping Penguins Bare* by Michael Carson and Caroline Stickland's *The Darkness of Corn*. Recent crime titles include Nancy Livingston's funny *Mayhem in Parva*, (her sixth tale of tax-inspector-turned-detective Mr Pringle), Simon Shaw's *Killer Cinderella* and Laurence Gough's *Serious Crimes*. And the backlist has always got Simon Brett and Michael Innes.

Gollancz science fiction (VGSF in paperback) has recent titles by, among many others, Arthur C. Clarke (*The Ghost from the Grand Banks*) and Greg Bear (*Queen of Angels*); Gollancz also have the new comic/fantasy star, Terry Pratchett: a recent title being *Eric* — about a demonology hacker living on Discworld. And again, the Gollancz backlist has got many titles by such as Aldiss, Heinlein, Asimov and Silverberg.

Gollancz are strong too on children's books. Among the very young children's titles are Shirley Hughes' lovely *Lucy and Tom's* . . . books. More importantly, they publish fiction series for 7–10 year-olds and for 11s-and-over. Recent "7–10" titles include Ann Cameron's *Julian, Secret Agent*, fourth in a light-hearted series about a young black boy and his friends. For the same age-group, the prolific Dick King-Smith has, as one of his latest books, *The Toby Man*. Recent "11+" titles include Nina Bawden's *The Outside Child*, Rosa Guy's *The Ups and Downs of Carl Davis the Third*, and Bob Shaw's *Killer Planet*. There are also titles within the 11+ list identified as for Young Adults. Peter Dickinson's gripping *Eva*, about a girl who finds she is unable to move or speak, is one such title; another is Robert Cormier's *Fade* —

about a boy who can disappear at will but isn't sure whether this is a good thing or not.

The Gollancz non-fiction list is fairly general, with specialist sub-series devoted to bridge-playing and, in a separate imprint, to fishing. They also have a number of impressive music books, eg *Stravinsky* by André Boucourechliev.

More generally, their recent books include "green" books, such as *The Greening of Medicine* by Patrick Pietroni, and biographies, including one of Katherine Hepburn by John Bryson. The list spreads widely.

Initial approach: for both fiction and non-fiction, they require a preliminary letter and a brief synopsis before receiving a manuscript. For fiction, they will then wish to see the complete manuscript; for non-fiction, they will discuss. Non-fiction books should preferably fit into a 60,000 to 120,000-word length. Gollancz are actively looking for new books — of the highest quality.

Decisions: can take up to three months.

Terms: usually, royalties of 10% on hardback price and 7.5% on paperback sale price for home sales; but not for children's picture book texts. Advances are variable.

GOWER PUBLISHING GROUP LTD

Gower House, Croft Road,
Aldershot, Hants GU11 3HR

T: 0252 331551

F: NIL	
NF: 300 (?)	5000
[1, 3, 6, 7]	

Non-fiction: Editorial Director

Founded in 1967, the Gower Publishing Group publishes mainly academic, professional and business management books. It has a very large list with several imprints — including Gower, Avebury and Scolar Press — and is expanding steadily.

The Gower list comprises practical professional books and higher academic works. Gower business titles include multi-authored management handbooks, the particularly well-received *Offensive Marketing: How to Make Your Competitors Followers* by J. Hugh Davidson, and *The Intuitive Manager* by Roy Rowan. Gower also publish books for professional librarians.

The Avebury list is almost exclusively devoted to research studies — on economics, international relations, philosophy, politics, law and sociology.

The Scolar imprint is for scholarly (of course) books primarily on art and architecture.

There is virtually no scope at all with any Gower imprint for non-specialist writers.

Initial approach: specialist non-fiction books should initially be offered to Gower in the form of a detailed synopsis, plus a statement of who the book is for, why there is a need for it, and why it should be written by the particular author.
Decisions: usually within a month.
Terms: are not revealed.

GRAFTON BOOKS

Division of HarperCollins Publishers
77–85 Fulham Palace Road,
London W6 8JB

T: 081–741 7070

F: 240 (25) · · ·
[L, G, C, S, R]
NF: 160 (35) · · ·
[1–4, 6]   H

Fiction: Fiction Editor
Non-fiction: Non-fiction Editor

Initially Granada Publishing, this publishing house was sold to Collins in 1983 and renamed Grafton in 1985. Today, it publishes in both hardback and paperback and is, to some extent, in competition with other imprints within the parent, HarperCollins Publishers. (Grafton books tend to be just a fraction more "popular" than those from Collins General Division. *See* page 46.)

Recent Grafton hardback fiction includes Eric Van Lustbader's *Angel Eyes*, *Dragon* by Clive Cussler, Nicola Thorne's *Bird of Passage*, *The Last Assassin* by Daniel Easterman, and Ray Bradbury's *A Graveyard for Lunatics*. From Betty Burton there is a joint hardback/paperback publication of *Consequences of War*. They have also recently published a number of multi-part fantasy books such as David Eddings' *The Ruby Knight* and Jack Vance's *Lyonesse III: Madouc*.

On the non-fiction side, recent titles range from David Pringle's *Ultimate Guide to Science Fiction* through John Butman's *Car Wars* and Dilip Hiro's *Black British, White British* to *Ball by Ball: The story of Cricket Broadcasting* by Christopher Martin-Jenkins. And there are the Punch books — *The Punch Book of Utterly British Humour* edited by Amanda-Jane Doran, and *Something Fishy: The Angle from Punch*, for example.

Grafton are actively seeking *good saleable* material in many categories; cookery, investigative works, travel/adventure, "name" biographies, military history, popular medicine, the paranormal, and film. (They also want TV tie-in material but to write that you probably need to be "tied-in" yourself.)

Initial approach: fiction — they prefer agented submissions but don't insist. Start with a preliminary letter and be prepared to follow up with the first 3–4 chapters of the novel plus a synopsis. For non-fiction, the usual synopsis plus assessment of need and market and author's credentials — following up swiftly with a couple of sample chapters.
Decisions: within about a month.
Terms: 10%/7.5% hb/pb royalties on list price home sales, or 10% of net receipts on exports. Advances vary.

ROBERT HALE LTD

Clerkenwell House,
45/47 Clerkenwell Green,
London EC1R 0HT

T: 071–251 2661

F: 300 (50)		700
[G, R, W]		
NF: 100 (35)		500
[1, 2, 3, 4, 5]		

Fiction: Robert Hale Ltd (not to any individual)
Non-fiction: Rachel Wright

Founded in 1936, Robert Hale has a vast fiction backlist, mainly *genre* fiction. It is a mainstay of many public libraries. The Hale non-fiction backlist is also large. It covers a very broad range: biographies to cookbooks, travel guides to "how to" books.

Hale's fiction list is divided into two: the general fiction list and the "light fiction" list. The general fiction list includes books by Pamela Street, Barbara Cartland, Jean Plaidy (over 70 novels in print), and James Hadley Chase. There are also books by Harold Robbins and Andrew Greeley (author of *Cardinal Sins*).

Beginning writers will be more interested in Hale's light fiction list. They publish nine *Rainbow Romances* (all contemporary) and eight *Blackhorse Westerns* each month. It is in these two series that most first novelists can best hope to achieve success with Hale.

The non-fiction list includes such recent titles as Richard Baker's biography *Marie Lloyd*, Erich Hoyt's nature book *Orca: The Whale Called Killer*, Betty Parkin's World War II memoir *Desert Nurse*, and *Witchcraft*, a personal account of witchcraft by practising witches Evan John Jones and Doreen Valiente.

There are a number of ongoing non-fiction series. One such is *The Illustrated Portrait of* . . . (various British counties and areas). Other series include: *Living in* . . . (France, Spain, etc.); *The Visitor's Guide to* . . . (London, Edinburgh, Scotland, etc.); and *The* . . . *Quotation Book* (Cook's, Lover's, Writer's).

Hale receive around 5,000 unsolicited manuscripts (fiction and non-fiction) a year — which they welcome. They produce a tip-sheet for romance writers; the ideal length for a Hale romance is about 45,000 words.

Initial approach: for fiction either the complete manuscript or the first three chapters plus a synopsis of the rest; for non-fiction a synopsis, a commentary on the need and market for the book, the author's credentials, and two sample chapters.
Decisions: usually four weeks but sometimes up to six.
Terms: these vary considerably from book to book and author to author. (It is believed that they pay lowish rates for their "light fiction" and near "industry standard" for general fiction and non-fiction.)

HAMISH HAMILTON

Part of the Penguin Books Group
27 Wrights Lane, London W8 5TZ

T: 071-938 3388

F: A* 40 (16)	300
C* 60 (17)	550
[L, G, C, K]	
NF: A* 50 (25)	880
C* no more	
[1, 2, 3, 4]	
* A=Adult, C=Children	

All adult — F/NF: Andrew Franklin (Publishing Director)
All children's — F/NF: Jane Nissen (Children's Director)

Founded in 1931, Hamish Hamilton were absorbed into the Penguin Books group in 1985. They have a large list, as big and interesting in children's books as it is for adults. They have a good name among writers and are offered nearly 3,000 manuscripts each year; they can afford to take only the best.

Past authors in the adult list — which leans slightly towards the "literary" end of the spectrum — include Nancy Mitford, Jean-Paul Sartre, Albert Camus and Truman Capote. Current titles include *Crucible of Fools* by M. S. Power, *The Photograph*, a much acclaimed first novel (a bestseller in France) by Jean Colombier and *No Talking after Lights* by Angela Lambert (whose first novel was shortlisted for the Whitbread prize).

Adult non-fiction is strong on biographies and general-interest titles. A recent biography is Katherine Frank's *Emily Brontë*. The breadth of the general-interest list is illustrated by recent titles: *Russian Roulette: Afghanistan through Russian Eyes* by Gennady Bocharov, *Rambling: On the Road to Rome* by Peter Francis Browne, and *My Kind of Jazz* by Brian Rust.

The children's list ranges from picture books such as *Princess Smartypants* by Babette Cole — a hilarious spoof tale describing Smartypants's struggle to remain a Ms — through a book of Jamaican short stories by poet James Berry, *A Thief in the Village* (Grand Prix Winner of the 1987 Smarties Prize), to the novel *Goggle Eyes* by Anne Fine — telling of a girl's gradual acceptance of a new man in her mother's life (Winner of the 1989 Carnegie Medal and the Guardian Children's Fiction Award).

Hamish Hamilton's children's non-fiction is no longer taking on new titles.

Initial approach: fiction or non-fiction, adult or children's — always — a preliminary letter and brief synopsis in advance of full or part manuscript.
Decisions: usually within a month.
Terms: royalties of 10% hb/7.5% pb on list price home sales, rising to 15% on hb sales. Adult book advances can be £2,000+.

HAMLYN PUBLISHING
(and PYRAMID BOOKS)

Subsidiary of Octopus Publishing Group
Michelin House, 81 Fulham Road,
London SW3 6RB

T: 071–581 9393

F: negligible*	
NF: 180 (N/A)	**500**
[1, 2, 3, 5]	
* Omnibuses or	
anthologies only	

Non-fiction: The Editorial Director

Hamlyn Publishing was founded in 1950 by Paul Hamlyn. Since then, there have been a series of complicated takeovers and mergers. Together with Pyramid (see below) and Bounty Books (the promotional imprint) it is now Octopus Illustrated Publishing, part of the Octopus Publishing Group within Reed International Books.

Hamlyn publish exclusively non-fiction books — glossy, general-interest, and with many illustrations, such as *The Complete Book of the Dog* by Joyce Robins — and offer little opportunity for the new writer. They have also published a useful series of *Help Yourself* Guides — even *How to get Published* by Neil Wenborn — but there is little or no scope for new, unsolicited, books in this, or any other Hamlyn, series. Hamlyn are more likely to go out and commission their books than to sift through what is offered.

Pyramid Books is a separate Octopus imprint, operating alongside Hamlyn Books. Books published by Pyramid are of more specialised general-interest: they cover the entertainment industry, with such recent titles as *The Hendrix Experience* by Mitch Mitchell and John Platt, and *Bugs Bunny* by Joe Adamson; and "name author" cookery, with books like *White Heat* by Marco Pierre White and Robert Lambert's, to me at least, irresistible-sounding, *Ultimate Chocolate Cookbook* — for chocaholics. Again though, unfortunately, not much scope for the new writer, unless you have really specialised knowledge.

Initial approach: if you really think you have a suitable idea for a Hamlyn or Pyramid book, try a written query.
Decisions: no information — probably within about a month.
Terms: no information.

HARRAP PUBLISHING GROUP
(including COLUMBUS BOOKS)

F: NIL
NF: . . . (. .)   **200**
[1, 2, 8]

Chelsea House, 26 Market Square,
Bromley, Kent BR1 1NA

T: 081–313 3484

Non-fiction: Jean-Luc Barbanneau (Publishing Director)

Harrap Ltd was founded in 1901 and made its name as a publisher of
dictionaries and educational books; then it expanded into self-study
courses, military and nautical books, biographies and business management books. In 1985 it took over Threshold Books and in 1986, the
general non-fiction publisher, Columbus Books. Then in mid-1989, W.
H. Allen bought their "general" list — all bar the reference books —
only to have it cut right back soon after, when Virgin's axe fell on WHA
(*see* page 187). Today, Harrap are virtually back where they started —
with a trimmed down but expandable reference and educational list. They
have in fact absorbed the children's educational list of Burke Publishing
Company.
   There is however, little scope for the "first-time" writer with Harrap.
What scope there is, is mainly in travel or educational books. Recent
new educational books include Anna Nyburg's *French for Fun* and Susan
McDougal's storybook approach to learning the multiplication tables,
Table Time. In travel books, there are recent titles in the Rough Guides
series including *Nepal* by David Peel and *Kenya* by Richard Trillo.
   Or maybe you can think of an idea for a new dictionary? Tony Potter
and Evelyn Goldsmith have just produced a 1,000-word illustrated *French
Dictionary* — for 5-year-olds and over.
   A biography of a past or present world leader (written for young adult
readers) is also a possibility; these books, taken on from Burke, are each
112 much-illustrated pages long; recent subjects have included *Oliver
Cromwell*, *Tenzin Gyatso: The Dalai Lama*, *Thatcher*, and *Queen Victoria*. The field looks open with that variety!

Initial approach: no advice, but I suggest that if you think you have a
Harrap-style book in you, you write and enquire if they might be
interested first.
Decisions: usually within a month, but can be quicker.
Terms: not known.

HEADLINE BOOK PUBLISHING PLC

Headline House
79 Great Titchfield Street,
London W1P 7FN

T: 071–631 1687

F: 260 (25)		700
[G, C, S, R]		
NF: 40 (35)		200
[1, 2, 3, 4, 5]		H

Fiction and non-fiction: The Editorial Department

Founded in 1986, Headline is growing fast; it aims straight at the very large "popular" book market and publishes in both hardback and mass paperback, often simultaneously. The backlist contains 900+ titles divided roughly 75% fiction, 25% popular non-fiction.

The fiction list includes many big name authors, and many new ones too: Headline is building a strong cadre of professional authors. Big names include medieval thriller-writer Ellis Peters with the *Brother Cadfael* books, and Dean R. Koontz (*Watchers*). There are also already four "glitzy" titles — *Riches, Scandals, Temptations* and *Enticements* — from the pen of new "name" Una-Mary Parker.

Among other new names are Sally Quinn, with the best-selling *Regrets Only*, and Unity Hall, with *The Rose and The Vine*. Fellow Allison & Busby author Donna Baker (author of *How to Write Stories for Magazines*), new to Headline, is now writing her second three-volume saga; the first, The Glassmakers, consisted of *Crystal, Black Cameo* and *Chalice*; the first book in her next saga, The Carpetmakers, has recently been published — *The Weaver's Daughter*.

The fiction list overall is strong on sagas (sagae?), thrillers and SF/fantasy books. When the W. H. Allen fiction list was so drastically cut back (*see* page 187), Headline took on several of their more popular authors, such as the prolific Tessa Barclay.

The Headline non-fiction list is just as strong. Many of the titles are illustrated; all are determinedly popular. There are books on wine and books on food; there are real-life crime stories; and there are books by and about personalities.

Initial approach: Headline prefer fiction to come through an agent but will consider unagented submissions — send the complete manuscript plus evidence of writing experience. For non-fiction, the usual detailed synopsis, justification of book and author, and sample chapters.
Decisions: usually within one month.
Terms: Headline are signatories to the Society of Authors/Writers' Guild Minimum Terms Agreement. They pay good but varied advances.

WILLIAM HEINEMANN LTD

Subsidiary of Octopus Publishing Group
Michelin House,
81 Fulham Road, London SW3 6RB

T: 071–581 9393

F: 40 (5)	· · ·
[L, G, R, C]	
NF: 40 (20)	· · ·
[1, 2, 3]	

Fiction and non-fiction: The Editorial Department

William Heinemann founded his publishing house in 1890; since then, although it has operated within a variety of business regimes, it has retained its individuality and grown apace. It is now part of the Octopus Group, which is owned by Reed International.

Another part of the Group, William Heinemann Educational, has a vast list of educational books (including the "Made Simple" series), selling widely throughout the world, which are not dealt with here; nor are Heinemann Young Books (*see* Octopus Children's books, page 123).

In the past, Heinemann published many now-famous authors, such as D. H. Lawrence, W. Somerset Maugham, and Nevil Shute. Their current fiction list includes such titles as *Lady Boss* by Jackie Collins and the latest book, *Trial by Fire*, by the "lady-in-waiting to such a queen of crime as Ruth Rendell", Frances Fyfield. Other recent crime/thriller titles include *Vespers* by "87th Precinct" author Ed McBain, *The Shadow of Elizabeth* by Michael Pearson, and a first novel, *Rush* by American writer Kim Wozencraft.

The Heinemann general non-fiction list includes such recent titles as V. S. Naipaul's *India*, Anthony Burgess's *You've had Your Time*, the second part of his autobiographical "confessions", and *Getting It Together*, the memoirs of ex-chairman of ICI, Sir John Harvey-Jones. But Heinemann also publish *Stick it up Your Punter: The Rise and Fall of The Sun* by Peter Chippindale and Chris Horrie, and Harry Shapiro and Caesar Glebbeek's *Jimi Hendrix: Electric Gypsy*.

Initial approach: fiction and non-fiction — Heinemann no longer read or accept for reading any unsolicited manuscripts from unpublished authors. **Terms:** for those they do publish, Heinemann pay royalties of 10% hb/7.5% pb on list price home sales. Advances vary with the book's potential.

HIPPO BOOKS
(and SCHOLASTIC HARDCOVER)

Imprint of Scholastic Publications Ltd
10 Earlham Street, London WC2H 9RX

T: 071–240 5753

F: 70 (5)	200
[K, S]	
NF: 30 (5)	100
[activity]	H

Fiction and non-fiction: Anne Finnis (Senior Editor)

The paperback imprint of Scholastic Publications (at Marlborough House, Holly Walk, Leamington Spa, Warwickshire CV32 4LS), Hippo Books were launched in 1980. They publish children's books only. There are picture books which range from an updated version of H. Werner Zimmerman's classic *Henny Penny*, through Chris Webster's *Betty the Yeti* (I couldn't resist including that title!) to Val Biro's *Tobias and the Dragon*. And there are dozens of John Cunliffe's *Postman Pat* books.

For older readers there are a number of series. *Streamers* are for 6–8 year old readers: a typical title could be *Broomstick Services* by Ann Jungman — modern witches delivering fast food, on broomsticks. For 8–10 year olds there is the *Jugglers* series: Angela Bull's *The Jiggery Pokery Cup* has the strong storyline — rivalry amongst a group of young children — typical of this series. *Hauntings* is a series for the 11+ reader: it includes Tessa Krailing's excellent *The Nightmare Man* and David Wiseman's *The Devil's Cauldron*.

Outside these series, there is the general fiction list; this includes such titles as Jean Ure's *Megastar*, the comical *Harriet And The Robot* by Martin Waddell and Angela Sommer Bodenburg's several *Little Vampire* books.

On the non-fiction side Hippo are strong on "activity books" which range from *The Brownie Fun Book* by Deborah Manley and *Christmas Games* by Karen King, to — almost inevitably — *The Postman Pat Travel Pack* by John Cunliffe. They are also building up their general non-fiction list with such recent titles as Kenneth Ireland's *True Ghost Stories* and Rupert Matthews' *Dictionary of Dinosaurs*.

Hippo occasionally publish poetry for children — but only anthologies. You would need to be very well known for them to consider a whole book by one poet.

Initial approach: for both fiction and non-fiction, Hippo would prefer authors to write in with a brief query before submitting material. They also say that they take *much* more seriously, submissions from agents.
Decisions: usually within about a month.
Terms: 7.5% royalties, and 5% for sales through the Scholastic Book Club — which is a very good "extra" market. Advances vary, but could be around £1,000.

HODDER & STOUGHTON LTD

47 Bedford Square, London WC1B 3DP

T: 071–636 9851

F: 85 (2)   200
[L, G, C, S, R, K]
NF: 50 (10)   150
[1, 2, 3, 4, 6]

Fiction and non-fiction: The Managing Editor

A large, but independent, publishing company, Hodder & Stoughton was founded in 1868 — and is still growing healthily. It took over the educational publisher Edward Arnold as recently as 1987. *New English Library* (*see* page 119) is a subsidiary.

Hodders are strong on general — popular — adult fiction, general children's fiction, suspense and crime fiction, general and biographical non-fiction, and — largely through the Teach Yourself books — "how to" and hobby books. They also include a strong religious book list.

Hodder's list of general fiction authors suggests how they have remained independent for so long. There are books by Jeffrey Archer, Jean M. Auel, Thomas Keneally, James Clavell, and Melvyn Bragg, to name but a few at random. Recent new titles include Janice Elliott's *Necessary Rights*, *Bimbo* by Keith Waterhouse, and Stephen King's *Four Past Midnight*.

In the crime/suspense list there are books by John le Carré, John Gardner, B. M. Gill (said to be chasing hard at the "Queen of Crime" heels of P. D. James and Ruth Rendell), Gavin Lyall, and Annette Roome, who won the Crime Writers' Association John Creasey Memorial Award for the best first crime novel. Recent titles include Michael Hartland's *The Year of the Scorpion* and the prolific John Gardner's new "Bond" book *Brokenclaw*. In the broad romance *genre* they have Jessica Stirling with, recently, *Wise Child*, Barbara Whitnell's latest, *Loveday*, and the many books by Phyllis A. Whitney, Hilary Norman and Elizabeth Adler.

Their children's fiction list includes Enid Blyton and the Asterix books — who needs more? They also have such titles as *A Christmas Child* by Melvyn Bragg and Brian Campbell, issued under their Knight imprint. As Lightning Books they have Christopher Pike's *Slumber Party*, Nicholas Walker's *Skating on Thin Ice* and Tim Scott, William Vandyk, and David Farris's *The Musketeers Adventure Agency*. They also issue a range of *Joke Books* — fiction or non-fiction?

A look at some of their recent non-fiction titles demonstrates the catholicism of the Hodder & Stoughton interests. They range from *The Discovery of the Bismarck* by Robert D. Ballard, through Brian Aldiss's *Bury My Heart at W. H. Smith's* to *Herbcraft* by Nerys Purchon. There is also an autobiography by the Dalai Lama; Sue Lawley has written up her recent *Desert Island Discussions*, and Christopher Andrew and Oleg Gordievsky have produced *KGB: The Inside Story*. And the religious list ranges widely with such recent titles as *Which One's Cliff?* by Cliff Richard and *Bad Samaritans* by Paul Vallely. The editors of the Teach

Yourself series also manage to keep on finding vacant slots in their already near-blanket coverage. There will always, it seems, be room for one more.

Finally, no review of Hodder & Stoughton's list would be complete without mention of their very successful *New International Version* of The Bible. (But unsolicited contributions to this are not appropriate.)

Initial approach: fiction — only through an agent. (You might perhaps just try writing to enquire, but whatever you do, don't send an unsolicited ms in out of the blue.) For non-fiction too, they much prefer submissions through an agent, but will consider "un-agented" submissions. These should consist of the usual detailed synopsis, assessment of need and market, a statement of the author's credentials, and two sample chapters.
Decisions: up to three months.
Terms: royalties basically 10% hb, 7.5% pb on list price home sales; advances vary.

HUTCHINSON BOOKS

Div of The Random Century Group Ltd

F: 40 (?)	
[L, G, C]	P
NF: 90 (?)	
[1, 2, 3, 6, 7]	

Random Century House,
20 Vauxhall Bridge Road,
London SW1V 2SA

T: 071–973 9750

Fiction and non-fiction: Editorial Director

Hutchinson Books was founded in 1887 but in 1985 became part of Century Hutchinson, and now, since 1989, a division of The Random Century Group Ltd. (For associate imprints, *see* Century Books, page 41.)

With such a long history, Hutchinson have the benefit of a massive and impressive backlist. They are somewhat stronger in non-fiction — certainly in terms of numbers — than in fiction. Recent fiction books include titles by such big "names" as Ruth Rendell, with her *Going Wrong*, H. R. F. Keating, with *The Iciest Sin*, Kingsley Amis, with *The Folks that Live on the Hill*, and John Wain, with *Comedies*. Len Deighton's spy novels also appear — frequently — in Hutchinson's fiction list. On the non-fiction side, recent titles include Tony Benn's *Diaries 1979–80*, *An American Life* by Ronald Reagan, and *The New Russians* by Hedrick Smith. A good mix of big names and topical subjects.

Hutchinson also publish some poetry. Recently they have published George MacBeth's *Trespassing*. And every year they publish *The Poetry Book Society Anthology*, currently edited by Fraser Steel.

Other imprints associated with Hutchinson include Muller Books and Radius. Muller, previously the old-established Frederick Muller, was relaunched within Century Hutchinson in 1988. It is a comparatively small list, concentrating on strong narrative fiction and show-biz associated titles, particularly biographies. Radius is a purely non-fiction list with an emphasis on politics and popular science.

Initial approach: fiction — first three chapters and a synopsis; non-fiction — detailed synopsis, author's credentials, and assessment of the market/need for the book, with two sample chapters available to follow on request.

Decisions: Hopefully, within about a month.

Terms: Century Hutchinson (hence Hutchinson) are signatories to the Society of Authors/Writers' Guild Minimum Terms Agreement — therefore royalties of 10% hb, 7.5% pb on list price home sales — with good "royalty jumps".

MICHAEL JOSEPH

Part of the Penguin Group
27 Wrights Lane, London W8 5TZ

T: 071–937 7255

F: 45 (5)		200
[L, G, C]		
NF: 55 (12)		200
[1–5 incl]		H

Fiction: Susan Watt (Publishing Director)
Non-fiction: Louise Haines (Senior Editor)

Founded in 1935, Michael Joseph became a part of the Penguin Group in 1986. They are a good "general" publisher, with a fine backlist of biographies and memoirs, of histories and of fiction. Among their past fiction successes they include books by John Masters, C. S. Forester and James Baldwin.

Recent fiction titles in their list include a new Miss Read book, *Friends at Thrush Green*, *Longshot*, the latest thriller from Dick Francis, and *Temples of Delight* by Barbara Trapido. A nice mix. And there are of course, many other recent titles — from Susan Hill, Claire Rayner, James Herriot and Norman Mailer, to name but a few.

Their non-fiction list covers all major non-specialist categories; recent titles span from *Trafalgar: Countdown to Battle 1803–1805* by Alan Schom and *Power of the Witch: A Witch's Guide to Her Craft* by Laurie Cabot with Tom Cowan, through *A Curmudgeon's Book of Love* edited by Jon Winokur and Jane Grigson's cookbook *Good Things*, to Denis Healey's *When Shrimps Learn to Whistle* and *Fat Man in Argentina* by Tom Vernon. All nice popular titles. Add to that the wit of Spike Milligan, in *It Ends With Magic* . . . and you have a really great mix.

Initial approach: fiction — complete manuscript; non-fiction — detailed synopsis, with assessment of need and market, and author's credentials, but initially, without the usual sample chapters.
Decisions: usually within about a month.
Terms: 10% hb, 7.5% pb royalties on list price home sales; advances vary considerably.

KOGAN PAGE LTD

120 Pentonville Road, London N1 9JN

T: 071–278 0433

F: NIL
NF: 200 (60)   1000
[4, 6, 7]

Non-fiction: Pauline Goodwin (Publishing Director —
Professional Books)
June Lines (Publisher — Trade Books)
Delores Black (Publisher — Education & Training Books

Kogan Page is an exclusively non-fiction publisher; founded in the late
Sixties, it now has a list of around 1,000 books. About 160 titles a year
were added in the late 1980s; they are now expanding at around 200 titles
a year.

The Kogan Page list is particularly strong in all aspects of business
management, eg. the effective marketing of a product or oneself, career
choices, communication skills and how to run a small business.

Many Kogan Page books are published in association with professional
institutions or commercial consultancies; some under the aegis of The
Daily Telegraph. The books are marketed hard, with display "spinners"
noticeable at most London main-line station bookstalls, larger High Street
bookshops and at airports worldwide.

One major series published by Kogan Page is the Better Management
Skills series, including such recent titles as *How to Develop Assertiveness*
by Sam Lloyd and *How to Write a Staff Manual* by Susan L. Brock and
Sally R. Cabell. Another series looks at the expanding opportunities of
the European Community, with titles such as *Setting up a Company in
the European Community* by Brebner & Co. and *1992: Strategies for the
Single Market* by James W. Dudley.

Other Kogan Page series include their Careers series (One title I
particularly noticed here was: *100 Part-Time Jobs for Mothers* by Christine Green. They also have series such as: Books for Teachers, New
Developments in Vocational Education, and Practical Trainer. Not all
their books are management-oriented.

If you really *know* about any aspect of management, or about a particular career, or about some aspect of modern technology, you could well
have a Kogan Page book in you. The scope of the Kogan Page list is
clearly defined but, within that, ranges wide. Among the well-known
authors in their list are John Fraser-Robinson and John Adair.

Initial approach: preferably — synopsis, statement of aims and objectives,
detailed appraisal of potential market for the book, and two sample
chapters. They particularly advise authors to discuss a book with them
before writing it.
Decisions: usually within a month.
Terms: royalties 10% hb, 7.5% pb on list price UK sales paid twice
annually; advances sometimes reach £2,000.

LADYBIRD BOOKS LTD

F/NF: 110 (20)   550
[children's]

Subsidiary of Longman Group
Beeches Road, Loughborough,
Leics LE11 3HS

T: 0509 268021

All: Pat Ross (Editorial Administrator)

Founded in 1924, Ladybird Books first began to issue the familiar much-illustrated pocket-sized books for children in 1940. They were taken over by the Longman Group in 1971. Ladybird publish, very successfully, exclusively books for young children. Ladybirds are part of growing up. Ladybird books are sold in bookshops and High Street multiples — and are even "given away" with petrol. Many Ladybirds are educational, few are textbooks.

In the last few years the Ladybird list has changed its nature. Gone are the long series of history books, the Famous People; instead there are more shorter-run series. And they are now perhaps geared more towards the younger age range.

The 1990 catalogue starts with Activity Books for 3-year-olds and — different books — for 6-year-olds; it moves on through simple stories in French, and graded readers for 6–10-year-olds to the Puddle Lane Reading Programme, all of which books are written by Sheila McCullagh. Then there are several starting-to-read series. For slightly older readers there are Well Loved Tales and Children's Classics. But Ladybird don't want unsolicited manuscripts for children's fiction.

Ladybird are however, willing to consider suggestions for new non-fiction titles — within existing series. Ongoing series include: Learners (6–9 age group) with titles like *Space*, *Dinosaurs*, and *Ecology*; Science (8+) including *Simple Chemistry* and *Weather*; Discovering (8+) with titles like *London*, *The Natural History Museum*, and *The Story of Madam Tussaud*, Achievements (10+) covering *Flight*, *Space*, and *Canals*; History of the Arts (10+) including the two-book *Lives of the Great Composers*. There are also a series of Bible Books published with the Scripture Union.

If you think you can produce a Ladybird book, Ladybird would be happy to consider the proposal. But don't hold your breath, most books are commissioned.

Initial approach: non-fiction only — synopsis, proposed "series-home", readership age, author's credentials and two sample chapters.
Decisions: no advice available.
Terms: no information.

LAWRENCE & WISHART

144a Old South Lambeth Road,
London SW8 1XX

T: 071–820 9281

F: 1 (1)	13
["socialist"]	
NF: 13 (7)	200
[1, politics]	

Non-fiction: Sally Davison (Manager)

A small, independent, left-wing publisher, founded in 1936, Lawrence & Wishart are "interested in publishing books that make a contribution to political understanding of the 80s and 90s in Britain." They also publish Labour Movement history.

Their non-fiction list includes the collected published works of Karl Marx, Engels and Lenin. Coming more up-to-date, recent titles include a collection of essays on *Citizenship*, edited by Geoff Andrews and another collection, *Music and the Politics of Culture* edited by Christopher Norris. There is also a strong feminist side to the list with titles like *Women Workers and the Trade Unions* by Sarah Boston, and *Sweet Dreams — Sexuality and Popular Writing* edited by Susannah Radstone.

The Lawrence & Wishart fiction list is very small, consisting largely of "socialist fiction" reprints; new book mss are not wanted.

If you are competent to write in the very specialised area of Lawrence & Wishart's interests, they are always interested in seeing new non-fiction book proposals. They are also "trying to develop cultural politics and the politics of race" — submissions in this area are very welcome. Any non-fiction book for them should preferably be at least 50,000 words long. They are offered around 40 non-fiction books a year.

Initial approach: non-fiction, detailed synopsis and justification of book and author, plus two sample chapters.
Decisions: usually take about three months.
Terms: royalties of 10% hb and 7.5% pb on list price; advances are negotiable.

LION PUBLISHING PLC

Peter's Way, Sandy Lane West,
Oxford OX4 5HG

T: 0865 747550

F: 10 (4)	85
[G, S, K]	
NF: 70 (14)	300
[1, religious]	

Adult fiction: Pat Alexander (Editorial Director)
Adult non-fiction: Lois Rock (Editor)
Children's Fiction & non-fiction: Su Box (Editor)

Founded in 1971, Lion is a specifically Christian book publisher, offering religious books for adult and children's reading. Their books are intended for the general — international — public; they are addressed to a popular, rather than academic or church, readership.

Among their fiction titles Lion are particularly pleased with Stephen Lawhead's books; his *Pendragon Cycle* weaves together the legends of Arthurian Britain and the lost Atlantis for adult readers. A recent adult fiction title — not by the prolific Lawhead — is John L. Moore's cowboy tale *The Breaking of Ezra Riley*.

Stephen Lawhead has also written several children's books for Lion, including a new series of "Riverbank Stories". Among other recent children's fiction books are *Nick & Co. to the Rescue* by Bob Croson, in his "Nick & Co." series, and Jenny Robertson's *Branded!*, the tale of a Scottish slave on the run in Rome.

The non-fiction list ranges wide. It includes *Here I Stand*, a biography of Martin Luther by Roland Bainton, and a Lion Handbook *The History of Christianity* — a "one-stop reference book". A recent historical biography is Bob Holman's biography of the socialist and Christian campaigner George Lansbury, *Good Old George*. There is also Michael Poole's *Guide to Science and Belief*.

Another notable recent Lion non-fiction title is Brenda Courtie and Margaret Johnson's GCSE textbook *Christianity Explored* — very easy to read and well presented. There is also an excellent series of Lion Factfinders (for 9-year-olds) including such titles as Barbara Holland and Hazel Lucas's *Caring for Planet Earth* and Meryl Doney's *Jesus*.

Lion are offered over 1,000 books and book proposals each year; less than one per cent are accepted. But they continue to look for "Christian books written specifically for the general reader and for sale in international general markets."

Initial approach: fiction — first few chapters and a synopsis. Non-fiction — preferably a written query first.
Decisions: within a month.
Terms: "normal royalties are paid, according to the work".

LONGMAN GROUP UK LTD

Longman House, Burnt Mill,
Harlow, Essex CM20 2JE

T: 0279 26721

F: 10 (1)   . . .
[K, Afro-Caribbean]
NF: 600 (250)   . . .
[6, 7, 8]

All (F & NF): David Lea (Manager: Copyright Department.)

Founded in 1724, the Longman Group is an international publishing company, operating in 75 countries. It is part of Pearson PLC, within which it is responsible for Ladybird Books (*see* page 102) and Pitman Publishing (*see* page 148).

Longman's areas of interest are broadly: education, ELT and dictionaries, medical, and business and professional publishing — virtually all non-fiction. They have long been renowned for their reference and educational books — at all levels. (Reprints of classroom classics apart, the small fiction list is Afro-Caribbean in origin and sales.)

A few of Longman's educational titles, chosen at random, give a feel for the breadth of the overall list: *The Italian Renaissance* by John Stephens, *Global Geomorphology* by M. A. Summerfield, *The Climax of Capitalism* by T. Kemp, and *The Novel Today* by Allan Massie.

Longman's ELT publishing includes, among many other titles, the "Blue Print" series by Brian Abbs and Ingrid Freebain. And there are all those dictionaries. In 1755 they first published Samuel Johnson's *Dictionary of the English Language*. (They have just re-issued a facsimile of this.) Today, they have the *Longman Dictionary of the English Language*, the *Longman Register of New Words* — and many others.

Through their Churchill Livingstone imprint, Longman publish medical books for the international market. Their *Grey's Anatomy* is the cornerstone of the list. Scope only for doctor writers. Their business and professional books include such titles as *The Children Act 1989: A Practical Guide* by Feldman and Mitchels and *West European Political Parties* by F. Jacobs. Very heavy.

If you are a real expert in almost any field though, Longman might well be interested in a book proposal.

Initial approach: for all non-fiction, Longman ask for a brief written enquiry first, outlining the subject, and including an assessment of the need and market for the book and the author's credentials.
Decisions: within three months.
Terms: will vary with the book and the potential market.

MACDONALD & CO LTD

Part of Maxwell Macmillan Pergamon
Publishing Corporation
Orbit House, 1 New Fetter Lane,
London EC4A 1AR

T: 071–377 4600

F: 45 (12)	**400**
[L, G, C, S, R]	
NF: 25 (12)	**200**
[1, 2, 3, 4, 5, 8]	**H**

All fiction and non-fiction: The Editorial Department

Founded just before World War II, Macdonald is now part of the Maxwell
Macmillan Pergamon Publishing Corporation. It publishes popular fiction
and non-fiction under its own imprint; largely sport-oriented non-fiction
under the Queen Anne Press imprint; and under the Optima imprint (*see*
page 124), books on alternative lifestyles and healthcare.

It has recently launched three more imprints, Orbit (science-fiction/-
fantasy), Scribners (quality fiction and non-fiction), and Scribners Crime
(crime and mystery fiction). Macdonald is also the parent of the paperback publishing imprints Futura (*see* page 74) and the recently acquired
Sphere (*see* page 178).

Recent additions to the mainstream Macdonald fiction list include
Jonathan Kellerman's *Time Bomb* and Beryl Kingston's *London Pride*.
Other top-selling authors in the Macdonald "stable" include Stephen
King and Lena Kennedy. The Orbit science-fiction/fantasy fiction list
includes such well-known authors as Iain M. Banks, Arthur C. Clarke
and the prolific Terry Brooks.

The Macdonald non-fiction list — relatively small, but growing —
includes such recent titles as *The Stephen King Companion* by George
Beahm and Dick Beresford's *The Uncensored Boy's Own*. Macdonald
also publish a few "coffee-table" type non-fiction books — such as *The
Decorated Doll's House* by Jessica Ridley.

In the new Scribners list, early non-fiction titles include James Gleick's
Nature's Chaos illustrated with the photographs of Eliot Porter. A part
fact, part fable story from Scribners is Edgar Hilsenrath's *The Story of
the Last Thought*.

Macdonald's children's list is now part of Simon & Schuster Young
Books (*see* page 174). Macdonald retained Enid Blyton's *Noddy* books —
but this list is complete.

Initial approach: fiction — preferably through an agent; if direct, just
the first few chapters plus a synopsis. Non-fiction — detailed synopsis,
assessment of market, author's credentials and two sample chapters.
Decisions: can take three months.
Terms: Macdonald do not disclose terms — but royalties are seldom less
than "the standard" (10% hb, 7.5% pb).

MACMILLAN LONDON
(and PAPERMAC)

Division of Pan/Macmillan Ltd
18–21 Cavaye Place, London SW10 9PG

T: 071–373 6070

F: 90 (6)	
[L, G, C]	
NF: 40 (25)	
[1–6 incl]	H
Papermac:	
NF: 40 (15)	

Fiction and non-fiction (incl. Papermac): Roland Philipps (Publishing Director), Jane Wood (Editorial Director)
Crime: Maria Rejt

The popular/mainstream imprint within the Macmillan Group, Macmillan London has a large backlist and publishes about 130 new titles each year (including around 50 a year in the crime list). They also publish about 40 new non-fiction titles a year in their associated paperback Papermac imprint (see below).

The fiction list of Macmillan London is strong, with authors such as Wilbur Smith, Rachel Billington, Rumer Godden, E. V. Thompson . . . and many others. Recent mainstream novels include *The Light Years* by Elizabeth Jane Howard, *The Bangkok Secret* and *Naked Angels* by Anthony Grey, and *Summer Secrets* by Jean Stubbs.

They also have a particularly strong crime list with books by Colin Dexter, Julian Symons and Simon Brett, as well as several top American crime writers. Recent crime novels include *'G' is for Gumshoe* by the American Sue Grafton (who is working through the alphabet: *'A' is for . . .*, *'B' is for . . .*, etc.), *Mrs Pargeter's Package* by Simon Brett, and *Crossbones* by Nancy Pickard. They also produce a "Crime Cheaps" series of low-cost reprints from the suspense list.

There may be scope for the first-time writer to break into the Macmillan list by way of the crime *genre* — unsolicited manuscripts from new crime writers are always welcome. The mainstream list is also open to the new writer — but the chances are significantly less.

The non-fiction list covers a wide scope. Among recent titles are *Macmillan* by Alistair Horne, *Moving the Mountain* (From the Cultural Revolution to Tiananmen Square) by Li Lu, and *The Estate* by The Duchess of Devonshire. There is also *The Bread Book* by Martha Rose Shulman and *The Making of Town Gardens* by Deborah Kellaway. The list is strong on autobiographies too — with *Miles* by trumpeter Miles Davis, and others by Roy Jenkins and Peter O'Toole — but you need to be a "name".

The Papermac imprint publishes exclusively non-fiction titles in a trade paperback format. The list is particularly strong in cookery, history, biography and music books. Recent titles include *Anton Mosimann's Fish Cuisine* by Anton Mosimann, *The Almost Meatless Diet* by Martha Rose Shulman, a re-issue of *The Golden Bough* by J. G. Frazer and a variety of tax guidance books — *The Touche Ross Tax Guide to . . .* by Bill Packer and other authors.

The Papermac list also includes the recent second edition of my own *The Successful Author's Handbook*. (This book is effectively, "How to sell — and then write — a non-fiction book"; it is essential reading for any non-fiction writer.)

Initial approach: fiction — full mss; non-fiction — synopsis, assessment of need, market and competition, writer's credentials and two sample chapters (all as in *The Successful Author's Handbook*).
Decisions: about four weeks in most cases.
Terms: royalties are usually 10% on home sales of hardback published price escalating to 15%. Trade paperback royalties are usually 7.5% on home sales list price. Advances depend on market potential.

THE MALVERN PUBLISHING CO LTD

Lloyds Bank Chambers, 18 High Street
Upton-upon-Severn, Worcs WR8 0HD

T: 06846 4408

F: 6 (6)	45
[L, G, R, C]	
NF: 3 (2)	15
[2, 3]	

Fiction and non-fiction: Tony Harold (Managing Director)

Malvern Publishing was founded in 1984 with the specific objective of publishing fiction by previously unpublished authors. Over the first few years it grew progressively — but perhaps a shade too fast for its financial resources to keep pace. Expansion had to be halted for a while, but the business has now been reorganised and new books are once again being taken on.

The Malvern fiction list is — sensibly — "popular"; most of the titles are thrillers or romances. At least one of the first novels published by Malvern has been picked up by a major publishing house and re-launched — Kate Rigby's *Fall of the Flamingo Circus* is now an Allison & Busby paperback. Other titles in the Malvern list include Chris Parker's horror story *Kyoki*, a number of thrillers by James Baddock, including *The Alaska Project*, and *Better Strangers*, an historical romance by Delia Ellis.

There is no doubt that Malvern provide an outlet for first novels which are always hard to place. And they seem able to make a commercial success of this.

They also publish a number of non-fiction books, including — appropriately — Fay Goldie's *How to Write Stories and Novels that Sell*. There is also Frances Brown's very successful illustrated history of British fairgrounds and their people, *Fairfield Folk*.

Initial approach: fiction — full manuscript; non-fiction — written query, briefly outlining the subject, treatment, and author's credentials — with the usual synopsis, assessment of market, need, etc., and sample chapters ready to follow.
Decisions: can take up to three months.
Terms: royalties of 10% hb, 7.5% pb on list price home sales; advances are variable.

METHUEN LONDON

Subsidiary of Octopus Publishing Group
Michelin House,
81 Fulham Road, London SW3 6RB

F: 100	
[L, G, C, S]	
NF: 70	
[1, 2, 3, 4]	**H**
Plays	

T: 071–581 9393

Fiction and non-fiction: Editorial Department

Methuen London is a general trade publishing house within the Octopus Publishing Group.

On the fiction side, Methuen London cover most general categories. Recent titles range from Leslie Thomas's *Bare Nell* and *The Magic Army* through Ursula Holden's *Help Me Please* to the science-fiction *Voyagers III: Star Brothers* by Ben Bova. TV scriptwriter David Nobbs has *The Complete Reginald Perrin* omnibus.

In non-fiction, recent titles range from trade leader Clive Jenkins' *All Against the Collar* and Brian Johnston's *Down Your Way* to *Remote People* by Evelyn Waugh and *Bulgakov and the Moscow Arts Theatre* by A. Smelyansky.

They are strong on humour too, with such recent titles as Victoria Wood's *Mens Sana in Thingummy Doodah*, *Holy Unacceptable* by Simon Bond, and *Mrs Weber's Diary* by cartoonist Posy Simmonds.

Methuen London also publish a lot of plays. Recent titles range from *The War Plays* by Edward Bond and *Plays One* by Mikhail Bulgakov to *Ten Tiny Fingers, Nine Tiny Toes* and *The Great Celestial Cow*, both by Adrian Mole's creator, Sue Townsend.

Initial approach: in all cases, a brief letter with a synopsis. Don't submit any "unexpected" manuscripts.
Decisions: no information — probably within six weeks.
Terms: no information.

MILLS & BOON LTD

Eton House, 18–24 Paradise Road,
Richmond, Surrey TW9 1SR

T: 081–948 0444

F: 300
[R]
NF: NIL

Fiction: The Editorial Department

Everyone knows about Mills & Boon, do they not? (But few of those who delight in ridiculing and criticising them ever read their books.) They are, of course, the world's best-known and most successful publishers of romantic fiction.

Founded in 1908 by the father of the present directors Alan and John Boon, and a long-since-departed Mr Mills, as a non-specialist publisher, Mills & Boon is now unique in its romantic specialism. Every budding writer of romance fiction dreams of having their book published by Mills & Boon. Many try; around 5,000 unsolicited manuscripts come in each year. All are carefully read, but only very few make the grade.

(It is sometimes suggested, and this must of course vary, that about ten per cent of Mills & Boon's unsolicited submissions are "encouraged" to try again, or to make some improvements. It is then said to be a very good year indeed for Mills & Boon if they actually find a dozen new writers.)

Certainly, many now well-established Mills & Boon writers wrote several books for them, each better than its predecessor, "serving their apprenticeship", before they got their first acceptance. Three or four rejected novels are about *par* before a Mills & Boon acceptance; thereafter three successful new books a year is not unusual. Mary Wibberly has one such success story; she tells about it in her excellent "how to" book *To Writers With Love* published by Buchan & Enright.

Mills & Boon are very generous with their help to aspiring writers. For an sae they will send a tip-sheet explaining their requirements: there is no formula but all of their books are written to set lengths (between 50,000 and 55,000 words — to fit into a standard 192 pages) and must obviously tell of a romance, convincingly, and with feeling. They want "good reads", not formula writing.

As well as the tip-sheet, they offer writers a 40-minute cassette called *And Then He Kissed Her*, which gives lots of advice on how to make a story come alive. (For this, send £4.95 to Mills & Boon at FREEPOST, P.O. Box 236, Croydon, Surrey CR9 9EL.) And writers' clubs and conferences up and down the country benefit from talks by Mills & Boon speakers. They really do want to find more *good* writers.

Not all Mills & Boon novels appear in paperback; most start in hardback and the majority then go on into paperback; the best ones are also taken up by the firm's overseas subsidiaries. Mills & Boon are loth to talk about how much money their writers make from their books, but if a title sells in several overseas markets as well as the UK, it will probably earn a very healthy sum. If Mills & Boon books were included in the weekly "best-seller" lists they would swamp the lists; many Mills & Boon writers are high in the list of PLR (*See* page 226) earners too.

Initial approach: they will consider either the full manuscript of a romance novel or the first three chapters plus a synopsis, whichever the author prefers. There is never a need to go through an agent — nor is one necessary after acceptance; Mills & Boon handle all rights worldwide. (They do not, of course, object to agents though.)

Decisions: despite the 5,000 manuscripts a year, they usually decide on unsolicited submissions within six to eight weeks.

Terms: they say, "Payment, or the system of payment, cannot be discussed unless and until a contract is offered."

MITCHELL BEAZLEY INTERNATIONAL LTD

F: NIL
NF: 28 (12)   120
[2, 3, 4, 5]

Part of Octopus Publishing Group
Artists House, 14–15 Manette Street,
London W1V 5LB

T: 071–439 7211

Non-fiction: Jack Tresidder (Publishing Director)

Founded in 1969, Mitchell Beazley is a prestigious publisher of illustrated non-fiction; the original family company joined the Octopus Group in 1987. Among their perhaps best-known titles are *The Joy of Sex* and *The World Atlas of Wine*. But they are equally well known for their *Pocket Guides* of which there arc now 70 currently available, many devoted to wine and food.

Auberon Waugh has said, "Mitchell Beazley have single-handedly provided the English speaking world with a complete wine library. . ." In addition to their wine Pocket Guides, they have many large-format, heavily illustrated, books on wine by such famous authors as Hugh Johnson, Michael Broadbent and Jancis Robinson.

Mitchell Beazley are also renowned for illustrated reference books, encyclopaedias, atlases etc., on interiors, gardening, crafts, photography, art and antiques. Their reference list is currently being expanded; they are now launching a series of non-fiction books for children.

Recent new titles include *The Art and Science of Wine* by James Halliday and Hugh Johnson, *Land and People* — a 1,600-page encyclopedia, Derek and Julia Parker's *Atlas of the Supernatural*, *Tolkien: The Illustrated Encyclopedia* by David Day and *The Art and Craft of Papier Mâché* by Juliet Bawden. There are also new editions of Miller's *Price Guides* and *Check Lists*.

Early titles in their new Young Books series include *Collecting for Keeps* by Judith and Martin Miller, *Tomorrow's Earth: The Squeaky-Green Guide* by David Bellamy, and *Amazing Space Facts* by Nicholas Booth.

Mitchell Beazley receive "a large number of unthought-out and unresearched ideas" for new titles each year — very few are accepted. For a book to interest Mitchell Beazley it must be well-researched, lend itself to the company's highly developed creative design skills, and have "an international dimension". That said, they welcome *appropriate* ideas for new titles.

Initial approach: a detailed synopsis, an assessment of need and competition, and the author's credentials.
Decisions: can take three months.
Terms: *either* a fee *or* royalties, usually based on net receipts and negotiated individually.

NEW ENGLISH LIBRARY

Subsidiary of Hodder & Stoughton Ltd
47 Bedford Square, London WC1B 3DP

T: 071–636 9851

F: 25 (0)	120
[G, C, R, S]	
NF: 5 (4)	20
[1, 3]	H

Fiction and non-fiction: Clare Bristow (Publisher)

A publisher largely, but not exclusively, of fiction, the New English Library has a sizeable, popular, list within the Hodder & Stoughton group. And some very well-known novelists — many American — are included in the list. NEL is also a major paperback publisher.

The backlist of NEL fiction writers includes Barbara Cartland, Robert Heinlein, James Herbert, Harold Robbins, and Dorothy L. Sayers. From time to time, they are reissued; they are all solid bestsellers. Generally, the list is stronger in the *genres* — specifically romance, horror, thrillers, and science fiction — than in "straight" fiction; it has a strongly popular image.

Recent crime/thriller titles include Ted Allbeury's latest, *Other Kinds of Treason* (a collection of short stories), David Mace's *Shadow Hunters*, and TV producer Trevor Barnes' *Dead Meat*.

A major SF release is the original, unexpurgated, edition of Robert A. Heinlein's bitterly satirical classic *Stranger in a Strange Land*. (It attacks religious explanations of faith and sexual relations based on jealousy. Major cuts were forced upon Heinlein when it was first published, in the 1960s.) And Piers Anthony has a new SF/fantasy, *Unicorn Point* — a sequel to *Robot Adept*. Stephen Gallagher's *Chimera* is a recent powerful story in the horror *genre* — as is F. Paul Wilson's *Reborn*.

Recent NEL romances include Rona Jaffe's *An American Love Story* and Belva Plain's *Harvest* — both writers are world-class bestsellers.

The small NEL non-fiction list is determinedly popular. Titles include show-biz biographies such as Ellis Amburn's *Dark Star: The Tragic Story of Roy Orbison* and Jim Brochu's *Lucy* (Lucille Ball) *in the Afternoon*. There are also cookery books — recently *Weight Watchers Carefree Cooking* by Ann Page-Wood.

Initial approach: fiction — NEL prefer manuscripts through agents — but they *will* consider "un-agented" submissions. Submit the first three chapters with a synopsis of the rest. For non-fiction the usual detailed synopsis, assessment of need and market, author's credentials, and two sample chapters.
Decisions: within three months.
Terms: 10% hb, 7.5% pb, both on list price home sales; advances vary with the book's potential.

NORTHCOTE HOUSE
PUBLISHERS LTD

> F: NIL
> NF: 50 (40)   200
> [2, 4, 6, 7, 8]

Plymbridge House,
Estover Road, Plymouth PL6 7PZ

T: 0752 705251/705255

Non-fiction: Roger Ferneyhough (Editorial Director)

A newly established publisher — founded in 1985 — Northcote House is actively seeking expert writers for their list, which is small but growing, and exclusively non-fiction.

The Northcote House list is strong in business and management textbooks, with about 45 books listed; titles range from *The Business of Banking*, through *The Crash and the Coming Crisis*, to *The Big Bang: The Financial Revolution in the City of London*. They also have a specialist travel imprint — Horizon Books — but this offers little opportunity for the new writer.

It is their new and fast-expanding *How To* series however, that is really of interest to the new writer. In addition to the 30-plus titles already published, a further 20 are in preparation. Titles include . . . *Do Your Own Advertising* by Michael Bennie, . . . *Survive Divorce* by Mary Kilborn, and . . . *Write for Publication* by Chriss McCallum. The *How To* books are all in paperback, from 25,000 to 70,000 words (96 to 224 book pages) long, with a lively style — plenty of diagrams, checklists, charts and cartoons (artwork is done by the publisher). Each book is targeted at a specific readership.

Northcote House require writers for the *How To* series to: "have first-hand experience of the subject; or be an experienced professional, consultant or teacher on the subject; or be an experienced specialist published writer on the subject." In a nutshell, they must really know the subject — not an unusual or unreasonable requirement.

In the future, Northcote House plans to concentrate increasingly on business education books, books for schools and colleges, and books on education management.

Initial approach: written enquiry, preferably with a detailed synopsis. And, "authors who put forward convincing sales arguments (for their book) are more likely to receive favourable consideration." Before agreement, the author will have to provide a more detailed outline and about 5,000 words of completed text.
Decisions: usually within a month — but can take three.
Terms: they now say, "by negotiation" — but their original "Author Kit" for the *How To* series mentions royalties of 7.5% *on net receipts*, paid annually.

OCTOPUS CHILDREN'S BOOKS

(Part of Reed International Books)

METHUEN CHILDREN'S BOOKS

A division of the Octopus Group
38 Hans Crescent, London SW1X 0LZ

T: 071–581 9393

```
F: . . . (. .)        . . .
[K]
NF: NIL
```


HEINEMANN YOUNG BOOKS

A division of the Octopus Group
Address as above.

T: 071–581 9393

```
F: . . . (. .)        . . .
[K]
NF:
[children's]
```


For both, all books: Editorial Department

Within the Octopus Publishing Group, the long-established children's lists of Methuen Children and Heinemann Young Books have been brought together with the children's books of Hamlyn and a new imprint, Buzz Books, as Octopus Children's Books.

It is not clear what direction the merged organisation will go and there is no information available on their future publishing programme.

Initial approach:
Decisions: no information
Terms:

OPTIMA

A division of Macdonald & Co Ltd
Orbit House, 1 New Fetter Lane
London EC4A 1AR

T: 071–277 4600

F: NIL	
NF: 32 (?)	175
[2, 3, 4, 5]	H

Non-fiction: The Editorial Department (Macdonald)

Launched in 1987 as a specialised, exclusively non-fiction, imprint of Macdonald (*see* page 109), Optima is growing healthily. It publishes books on modern and alternative lifestyles and healthcare — currently a (*green* and) booming area. But it is difficult to categorise the list beyond that broad description.

The only way to give an overall feel for the Optima list is to refer to typical titles, both backlist and recent.

There are Alternative Health titles such as Ursula Markham's *Hypnosis* and Gill Martin's *Aromatherapy*. There are Positive Health Guide backlist titles such as *Overcoming Arthritis* by Dr Frank Dudley Hart and *The Diabetic Kids' Cookbook* by Rosemary Seddon and Jane Rossiter. Recent Positive Health titles include *Living with Teenagers* by Dr Brenda Litner and *Herpes: What it is and How to Cope* by Dr Adrian Mindel and Orla Carney.

In the main part of the Optima list the titles range from Tony Crisp's *Dream Dictionary* and Michael Allaby's *Guide to Gaia*, through Jane Ward's *One Parent Plus: A Handbook for Single Parents* and Leon Chaitow's *Stone Age Diet: The Natural Way to Eat*, to *Green Parenting* by Juliet Solomon and *The Yin-Yang Cookbook* by Oliver and Michele Cowmeadow.

Recent titles continue to reflect the breadth of the Optima list. There are such titles as *The Condom Book for Girls* by Alison Everitt, *Green Dictionary* by Colin Johnson, and *Blitz: The Civilian War 1940–45* by Jane Waller and Michael Vaughan-Rees. And there is *How to Analyze Your Own Handwriting* by Patricia Marne.

There is, throughout the Optima list, a small but undoubted emphasis on "women's interests". And there are a few books of cartoons such as Ros Asquith's *Baby!*

Initial approach: non-fiction only — the usual — detailed synopsis, assessment of market/need, author's credentials and two sample chapters.
Decisions: can take three months.
Terms: In common with other Macdonald imprints, Optima will not disclose terms — but the royalties are seldom less than "the standard" (10% hb, 7.5% pb).

ORCHARD BOOKS

F: 55 (5)   136
[K]
NF: neglig.

Division of The Watts Group
96 Leonard Street, London EC2A 4RH
T: 071–739 2929

Fiction: Fiction Editor

Founded in 1985, Orchard Books specialises in children's fiction and picture books. (The associated publishing house, Franklin Watts, handles the non-fiction — *see* page 191.) The Orchard list ranges from board books, picture and novelty books, to fiction for all ages of children. The emphasis throughout is on illustrated books.

The toddler books include baby board books by Sian Tucker and books like Robin Kramer's lift-the-flap *Where's Baby* picture book. Novelty books include several by pop-up specialist Jan Pienkowski and the three-dimensional *Dinner with Fox* by Stephen Wyllie. An interesting recent picture book is the 32-page *A Dinosaur's Book of Dinosaurs* written by Roger Dinosaur and "edited" by Keith Brumpton.

Most of the fiction for younger readers (up to 10 years old) is in the Orchard Readalouds series, illustrated with line drawings. Recent Readalouds include Jill Bennett's *Jack Bobbin* and Rose Impey's *The Revenge of the Rabbit*. There is also *China Lee*, Sue Limb's first children's novel, which was shortlisted for the 1987 Whitbread Award.

Orchard Originals are trade paperbacks for readers of 10+ and are at least 128 pages long. Typical recent titles include *Finders, Losers* by Jan Mark (a "jigsaw puzzle" of a novel with six inter-related but separate stories), Jean Ure's *Cool Simon*, set in the top class at Woodside School, and *Big Trouble*, a strong story about personal relationships by Sue Limb.

Initial approach: for fiction, submit full manuscript.
Decisions: usually within about a month.
Terms: royalties 7.5% on list price; advances vary.

PETER OWEN LTD

73 Kenway Road, London SW5 0RE

T: 071–373 5628

F: 28 (0)	200
[L]	
NF: 20 (5)	180
[1, 2, 3]	

Fiction and non-fiction: Editorial Director

A much-admired small, independent firm, Peter Owen Publishers was founded in 1951. It has built up a prestigious reputation, mainly for the quality of its "literary" fiction but also for its biographies and memoirs. Among the famous authors who have been published by Peter Owen are Hans Christian Andersen, Herman Hesse, Yoko Ono, Jean-Paul Sartre and Muriel Spark. They also publish the work of Shusako Endo, one of Japan's greatest living writers and a contender for the Nobel Prize, and the Prize-winning Octavio Paz.

The Peter Owen fiction list is noteworthy for the number of translations and imported books it includes; among recent novels are *Confessions of Love* by the Japanese author Uno Chiyo and *Insect Summer* by one of Norway's best-known writers, Knut Faldbakken. (American writer Paul Bowles has more than a dozen books — fiction and non-fiction — in the Owen list: recently, his autobiographical *Two Years Beside the Strait.*) The fiction list also has many short story collections.

The Peter Owen non-fiction list is of interest for its biographies and memoirs of interesting, but less than famous people. *As It Happened* by journalist Edwin Tetlow and *Chamberet* — the story of a Jewish family in wartime France — by Claude Morhange-Begue are good examples of such books. Other Peter Owen "lives" are about better-known people: recent titles include *My Life* by Edith Piaf and *Anna Kavan* by Priscilla Dorr. They are also publishing a controversial biography of billionaire publisher Malcolm Forbes.

The publishers are always interested in seeing new manuscripts, both fiction and non-fiction, but emphasise that they only want outstanding literary work. They are offered around 300 unsolicited books or book proposals each year and accept very few. (But they will be publishing several particularly good first novels in 1991.)

Initial approach: preferably through an agent, but if not, a letter of enquiry first, followed by sample chapters and a synopsis, rather than a complete unsolicited manuscript. And don't forget the SAE!
Decisions: within about a month.
Terms: first-time authors can expect industry-standard royalties of 10% on hardback sales and/or 7.5% on paperback sales. Advances depend on book and author.

OXFORD UNIVERSITY PRESS

Walton Street, Oxford OX2 6DP

T: 0865 56767

F: NIL
NF: 1,000 (?)   . . .
[1, 2, 3, 6, 7, 8]

Non-fiction: The Oxford Publisher

The Oxford Univeristy Press has a huge list of academic and educational books; its current general stock catalogue fills over 500 pages of Bible-thin paper — but excludes the Bibles themselves, which are in a separate list; the books are catalogued in Dewey classification sections — and very few sections are missing or empty.

The OUP list is so vast that it is virtually impossible to single out any section, and certainly any title, for specific mention. However, apart from the Literature (Dewey 800) section, which includes a large number of classic titles — by authors from Cicero to Robbie Burns and from Alfred Lord Tennyson to Henry James — the largest section is probably Social Sciences (Dewey 300). And then there are all the school textbooks — on any and every subject known to teachers worldwide.

But Oxford do publish some somewhat more "ordinary" books too. Among recent general non-fiction books are *The People's Peace: British History 1945–1989* by Kenneth O. Morgan, a biography, *Mrs Humphry Ward: Eminent Victorian, Pre-Eminent Edwardian* by John Sutherland, and *Anecdotes of Modern Art: From Rousseau to Warhol* by Donald Hall and Pat Corrington Wykes. But they are all still fairly "heavy".

Oxford University Press cannot be thought of as a sensible target for the beginning, non-academic, writer to submit work to. It is neither a "general" nor a popular publisher — it is a university press.

Initial approach: if you think you can produce the right type of non-fiction book for OUP, send them the customary detailed synopsis, assessment of need, market and competition, and author's credentials, plus a couple of sample chapters.
Decisions: they cannot specify a time for responding.
Terms: royalty rates are not specified; these depend on the type of book, as do whether or not they will pay any advance.

PAN BOOKS LTD

Division of Pan/Macmillan Ltd
18–21 Cavaye Place,
London SW10 9PG

T: 071–373 6070

F: 300 (40*)   1000
[L, G, R, C, S, K]
NF: 200 (100*)   800
[1, 2, 3, 4, 5, 6, 8]   H
* but *not* from unsolicited MS

All unsolicited manuscripts (fiction or non-fiction, adult or children's):
Unsolicited Manuscripts Editor

Pan Books was founded in 1944 and quickly established itself as a major paperback publishing house. Ian Fleming's "Bond" books undoubtedly helped them to establish their place in popular literature. For many years, Pan was jointly, and equally, owned by Macmillan, Collins and Heinemann — and able to choose titles from these three lists. Today, it is wholly within the Macmillan "empire" — and buys in titles.

Among well-known books published in Pan there are the ever-popular thrillers of Wilbur Smith and Jack Higgins, Tom Sharpe's outrageously funny books, *Wilt*, *Porterhouse Blue*, and *Blott on the Landscape*, for example, and Leslie Thomas's *Virgin Soldiers*, *The Love Beach*, *Tropic of Ruislip*, etc. — all hilariously funny. Pan is also strong on fantasy novels. A few years ago there was Julian May's 4-volume "Saga of the Exiles". And there are Douglas Adams' books: *The Hitch-hiker's Guide to the Galaxy* — and all the rest.

Pan's non-fiction list is also well thought of. How could it fail to be, with writers such as James Herriot, Madhur Jaffrey, Robert Hughes and Alvin Toffler. They also have some excellent books on management, on which I, and many others, "grew up".

Pan is the general-interest popular imprint; others include the more literary Picador imprint, for the best of international writers, and the children's imprint, Piccolo/Piper.

It has to be remembered that Pan are basically a reprint paperback publisher; nearly all of their titles have already been published in hard-back by another publishing house. They are always interested in seeing new writers' work, but caution against over-optimism. They accept very very few unsolicited submissions — less than one per year.

Initial approach: fiction — preferably, through an agent. For non-fiction books, they prefer to receive just a written query outlining the content.
Decisions: can take three months.
Terms: royalties at 7.5% of list price on paperback sales; advances vary but could be as much as £3,000 for a novel and £1,500 for a non-fiction title.

PANDORA PRESS

Imprint of HarperCollins Publishers (at the time of going to press was up for sale)
77–85 Fulham Palace Road,
London W6 8JB

T: 081–741 7070

F: 10 (5)	50
[L, G, C]	
NF: 30 (20)	200
[1, 2, 3]	

Fiction and non-fiction (except health): Philippa Brewster (Editorial Director)
Health and non-fiction: Candida Lacey (Senior Editor)

Pandora Press is a publisher of up-to-the-minute fiction and non-fiction — written by today's women writers for today's women. All Pandora writers are women.

Pandora was launched in 1983, as an imprint of Routledge & Kegan Paul; it was transferred to Unwin Hyman in 1988. It is now, since 1990, an imprint of HarperCollins Publishers.

Their modern fiction includes novels by Jeanette Winterson (who won the 1985 Whitbread Award for a First Novel with *Oranges are Not the Only Fruit*), Janet Frame, Kathy Acker and Jane Rule. They have also recently published a pair of novellas — *The Strawberry Tree* by Ruth Rendell and *Flesh and Grass* by Helen Simpson — under the title *Unguarded Hours: Exercises in Suspense*. Among their crime books, they publish, among other titles, the Kate Delafield mysteries of Los Angeles-based Katherine V. Forrest — her latest is *The Beverley Malibu*.

Note that 50% of their output can be first novels, but the competition is fierce: they receive about 2,000 unsolicited book offers a year, mostly fiction — they publish perhaps half a dozen. Recent first novels include titles by Hillary Johnson and Phyllis Burke.

Pandora's non-fiction list emphasises books that inform and entertain their readers, encouraging them to share the author's excitement in her subject. Their health and psychotherapy, biography, modern culture and reference lists are strong and developing. Typical recent Pandora titles include Jill Benton's biography *Naomi Mitchison: A Century of Experiment in Life and Letters*, *Erotica: An Anthology of Women's Writing* edited by Margaret Reynolds, *Bad Girls of the Silver Screen* by Lottie Da and the cartoon book *Babies!* by Ros Asquith.

Initial approach: fiction — first two or three chapters and a synopsis; non-fiction — the usual detailed synopsis, assessment of need and market, author's credentials, and two sample chapters.
Decisions: within one to two months.
Terms: "industry-standard" royalties of 10% hb/7.5% pb on list price home sales. Advances vary with potential.

PAN/MACMILLAN CHILDREN'S BOOKS

Division of Macmillan Trade Publishing Group
18–21 Cavaye Place, London SW10 9PG

T: 071–373 6070

Fiction and non-fiction: Michael Wace (Publishing Director)

In mid-1990, the Pan Children's Division and Macmillan Children's books were brought together into a single publishing division. The separate imprints remain. The Macmillan list is primarily hardback: it includes 32-page picture books (recent titles include *Say Hello, Tilly!* by Wendy Smith and *Mucky Moose* by Jonathan Allen), younger fiction for the 7 to 9 age group (eg *My Famous Father* by E. W. Hildick), older fiction and non-fiction. For the over–12s, recent titles in the paperback Limelight series include *The Broken Bridge* — a tale of self-discovery, of a mixed marriage, and the arrival of a unknown-of brother — by Philip Pulman, and *Secrets* — exploring the problems of anorexia nervosa — by Sue Welford.

Also under the Macmillan imprint is the well-established paperback picture book list, Picturemac; recent titles here include *A Rose for Pinkerton* by Steven Kellogg and *Pookins Gets Her Way* by Helen Lester, illustrated by Lynn Munsinger.

The Pan list is primarily a popular paperback list with particular strengths in fiction (the Picture Piper, Young Piper and Piper imprints) and non-fiction (the Piccolo imprint). There are also home learning books.

Recent Picture Piper titles include *Rex, The Most Special Car in the World* by Victor Osborne; recent Young Piper titles include Terence Blacker's *You're Nicked, Ms Wiz* and *In Control, Ms Wiz?* Piper titles include the 1989 Smarties Award-winning *Blitzcat* by Robert Westall and *Gander of the Yard* by David Henry Wilson. A recent non-fiction title in the Piccolo imprint was *100 Great Games: The Remix* by Sutherland & Gross. They have also recently brought out *The Really Revolting Puzzle Book* by Scoular Anderson.

Initial approach: fiction — synopsis and sample pages; picture books — text and photocopy of sample artwork; non-fiction — synopsis only.
Note — the publishers emphasise that they accept very few unsolicited books.
Decisions: "allow at least a month".
Terms: no information.

PENGUIN BOOKS

27 Wrights Lane, London W8 5TZ

T: 071–938 2200

F: 225 (0)	*****
[L, G, C, S]	
NF: 200 (?)	*****
[1–8]	**H**
	***** **see text**

All: Editorial Director, Penguin Books

Penguin Books is the largest paperback publisher in Britain and one of the best-known in the world. It was founded by Sir Allen Lane in 1935 to provide the British public with good books for sixpence a copy. The first titles were all reprints of successful hardback books. Allen Lane's idea took off — and changed the reading habits of the British public.

The Penguin list now runs into many thousands of titles; a current Penguin stocklist is a 52-page book with three columns of titles per page — and the Puffin list (*See* page 151) fills a further 16 similarly crowded pages. Penguin fiction still consists almost entirely of reprints but the non-fiction list — around half of the total — contains about fifty per cent original titles. Each year, they are offered around 4,000 unsolicited manuscripts.

Apart from their "general" and "literary" fiction, Penguin publish a number of crime and science fiction/fantasy titles too. Current Penguin authors range from Graham Greene and John Mortimer via Anthony Burgess and John Wyndham to Martin Amis, Ruth Rendell (writing as Barbara Vine) and Sara Paretsky. Top writers undoubtedly *like* to be in Penguin. And, of course, if you want a copy of just about *any* classic book, Penguin have it — from Homer via Tolstoy to George Orwell. They have humour too: the first volume of Spike Milligan's family history, *It Ends With Magic*, for example.

Recently they have successfully started publishing "graphic fiction" — comic books by any other name. They are the first mainstream publisher in this field; they are going for it in a big way.

On the non-fiction side they cover the lot: biography, memoirs, history (a strong section), art, architecture, business management, philosophy, politics, economics (also strong) psychology, science — and "general" non-fiction. You name it, Penguin have a book on it.

They publish poetry too — but say, "we are likely to approach poets, rather than the reverse."

Initial approach: as a reprint house for fiction, agented submissions are most likely to achieve success. For non-fiction, send a short written query first.
Decisions: within about six weeks.
Terms: for new works, 7.5% on home sales; advances vary.

PERGAMON PRESS PLC

Headington Hill Hall,
Oxford OX3 0BW

T: 0865 794141

F: NIL
NF: 120 (60)   4000
[5, 6, 7, 8]

Non-fiction: The Editorial Director — subject area

Pergamon Press was founded in 1948 by Robert Maxwell. It specialises in publishing "heavy" academic texts — but if you can meet the academic requirements they welcome new writers and new ideas.

To get a good idea of their needs it is only necessary to look through their list of forthcoming titles. Titles are classified under: Life Sciences and Medicine, Engineering and Materials Science; Physical Sciences; Social and Behavioral Sciences; and Chess.

A few of the more esoteric titles that caught my eye were: *Intercapsular Cataract Extraction* edited by E. S. Rosen; *Rational-Emotive Therapy with Alcoholics and Substance Abusers* by Albert Ellis and others; *Designing & Applying Recognised Techniques to Small Businesses* (This is a 10-volume set selling at £125 per set — think of the royalties on each sale) by *Trace*, a Wigan College of Technology company; and *Would the Insects Inherit the Earth?* by J. C. Greene and D. J. Strom.

But there are a few books more within reach of us ordinary mortals. Pergamon are strong in books about chess: *Play the Catalan, Volume 2* by J. Neishtadt, and L. Alburt's *Chess by Numbers* are two typical titles. And, classified by Pergamon as "of general interest", there is *Chernobyl*, a comprehensive history of the first 18 months by R. F. Mould.

If you come from the world of academe, or are a chess master and want to get your knowledge into print, then Pergamon may well be interested in an idea for a book. But there is very little scope here for the generalist writer.

Initial approach: non-fiction only, a detailed synopsis, accompanied by an assessment of the need and market for the book, an appraisal of the likely competition, and your author's credentials; ideally, this should be accompanied by a couple of sample chapters.
Decisions: usually within a month.
Terms: royalties will usually be the "standard" 10% hb/7.5% pb but may vary for a book with limited interest; advances too will vary with the market potential and the book price.

2 Kelly Gardens,
Calstock, Cornwall PL18 9SA

T: 0822 833473

Poetry: Harry Chambers (Publishing Director)

Founded in 1976, Peterloo Poets is — as the name implies — a publisher solely of poetry. The best-known work in their current list is U. A. Fanthorpe's *A Watching Brief*. Among their recent poetry-collection titles are *Nobodies* by Anna Adams and, for children (but equally suitable for adults), *The Mad Parrot's Countdown* by the award-winning poet John Mole.

Like all small poetry publishers, Peterloo Poets are swamped with submissions: they get over a thousand manuscripts sent to them each year — and make a plea for poets to send not just the stamps for return postage, but also an adequately-stamped, full-sized, self-addressed envelope. That apart, they are not too fussed as to just how the book manuscript is submitted — either a few samples first, or the full book straight away.

Peterloo Poets are always keen to find good new poets. They say that they "look forward to receiving poetry submissions from people who actually *read* poetry". They particularly advise poets thinking of submitting their work to any publisher, to go out and buy at least one book of poems from that publisher's list, in order to see what sort of poetry is appropriate.

The Publishing Director, Harry Chambers, also commends budding poets to read the section on *Poetry Publishing Today* in the current *Writers' & Artists' Yearbook* (A. & C. Black).

Initial approach: no preferences.
Decisions: take an average of three months.
Terms: royalties of 10% on paperback sales; advances on a first volume are seldom, if ever, more than £50.

PHILLIMORE & CO LTD

Shopwyke Hall,
Chichester, West Sussex PO20 6BQ

T: 0243 787636

F: NIL
NF: 50 (35)   750
[1]

Non-fiction: Noel Osborne (Editorial Director)

A small specialist publisher — of British local and family history —
Phillimore are happy to consider proposals for appropriate non-fiction
books. In an average year they receive about five hundred non-fiction
submissions. (A strictly non-fiction house, they also receive twenty or
more fiction manuscripts each year. So much for writers' market
research!)

They are particularly interested in considering proposals for books to
fit into their series of *Bygone . . .* books, which look at British towns
through many old photographs.

Typical recent titles, taken at random from their comprehensive list,
include the history of a great Cumbrian land-owning family, *The Lowther
Family* by Hugh Owen (winner of the 1990 Portico Prize), *Bygone Not-
tingham* by Christopher Weir, *Brent: A Pictorial History* (a near-standard
160 well-captioned illustrations within a 128-page large-format book) by
Len Snow, and *A History of County Durham* (in their profusely illustrated
Darwen County History series) by Douglas Pocock and Roger Norris.

Non-fiction books for Phillimore should be aimed at a final length of
between 30,000 and 120,000 words. They are very willing to discuss
appropriate book proposals at an early stage, to help get them right.
Eventually though, they will require the customary detailed synopsis and
sample chapters. You will need to have very considerable and detailed
knowledge of your subject. And do look carefully at some of their existing
books before approaching them.

Initial approach: ideally, a detailed synopsis plus a well-researched and
logical statement of who the book is intended for, why there is a need
for it, what the competition is like, and why you are the best author to
write this particular book; and two sample chapters.
Decisions: if expert outside opinion has to be sought, this can take three
months.
Terms: royalties usually 10% hb/7.5% pb on published price. Advances
are not normally offered.

PIATKUS BOOKS

Judy Piatkus (Publishers) Ltd
5 Windmill Street, London W1P 1HF

T: 071–631 0710

F: 80 (8)	300
[G, C, R]	
NF: 60 (26)	220
[1, 3, 4, 6]	

Fiction: Judy Piatkus (Publisher)
Non-fiction: Gill Cormode (Editorial Director)

Founded in 1979, Piatkus Books is a medium-sized, fast-growing, independent publishing house with a backlist of over 1,000 titles. Piatkus Books are offered around 2,000 new books each year and they are currently publishing 60 non-fiction and 80 fiction titles a year — including a number (about 10%) of first novels.

The fiction list concentrates largely on commercial novels, family sagas, historical and contemporary romances, crime, horror, and blockbusters. Among "mainstream" Piatkus writers are the best-selling American novelists Barbara Michaels (recently *Into the Darkness*) and Jennifer Wilde. Leading British novelists include Malcolm Ross (the recent *A Woman Alone* is his fifth Piatkus novel) and Elizabeth Walker, with *Conquest*.

Piatkus is growing apace too, with crime books and thrillers from such authors as Elizabeth Peters and Margaret Duffy; recent titles include Eileen Dewhurst's *A Nice Little Business*, Erica Quest's *Cold Coffin* and Susan Kelly's *Time of Hope*.

On the non-fiction side, Piatkus is strong on practical and how-to books, cookery, women's interests and "mind, body and spirit". The business book side of the Piatkus list is also developing very strongly. Major titles in the business list include *What They Really Teach You at The Harvard Business School* by Frances Kelly and Heather Mayfield Kelly, *Powerspeak* by Dorothy Leeds, and *The Complete Time Management System* by Christian H. Godefroy.

The Piatkus backlist includes many more major titles covering health and beauty, parenting, and sex. It also includes *The Curry Club* recipe books by Pat Chapman.

Initial approach: fiction — either a complete manuscript, or the first 3–4 chapters plus a synopsis. Non-fiction — preferably a detailed synopsis, a "justification" for the book, and the author's credentials, with sample chapters ready to follow. Aim at a minimmum length of 45,000 words for non-fiction.
Decisions: usually within about a month.
Terms: usually 10% hb, 7.5% pb on list price. Advances are negotiable.

PICCADILLY PRESS

5 Castle Road, London NW1 8PR

T: 071–267 4492

F: 27 (1)	27
[K]	
NF: 4 (2)	4
Fact books	H

Fiction and non-fiction: Ruth Williams

A small, specialist, publishing house, founded in 1983, Piccadilly Press publishes exclusively hardback children's books, mainly fiction. Their list is in three sections: picture books for the under-5s, stories for the 5–8 year old, and fiction for readers aged 8–12. Most Piccadilly books are amusing and light-hearted.

Stories for the 5–8 year old group should be around 5,000 words long. Most such Piccadilly books are in series: several books *by the same author, about the same character(s)*. Piccadilly like to get several follow-up books once they commission the first of a series. Terrance Dicks' *David & Goliath* series (recently, *Teacher's Pet*) and Tony Bradman's *Bluebeards* series (recently, *Search for the Saucy Sally*) are typical Piccadilly series.

Potential Piccadilly books for the 8–12 year old reader should be around 10,000 words long — ghosts, parents, friends, and sports are suitable subjects for this age group.

Quite recently, they have also started to publish non-fiction. This is a difficult area for an author to get right, so they prefer a query letter before anything further.

They might also be willing to consider *relevant* books of poetry (for children) — but again, this is a new venture for them.

Although they are a very small publishing house of not many years' standing, they already receive some 100 unsolicited book manuscripts per year: the chances of actually breaking in are fairly small.

Initial approach: fiction — a written query with a couple of chapters and a synopsis; non-fiction — just the query letter first. They look with much greater favour on agent-submitted manuscripts: the book has already passed one test, and the agent will know which manuscript might be suitable for which publisher.
Decisions: usually within one month; only very occasionally will they take longer.
Terms: 10% of list price on hardback sales in the home market; they do not publish paperbacks. Advances will vary considerably, depending on the length and their assessment of the saleability of the book.

PITMAN PUBLISHING

Subsidiary of Longman Group
128 Long Acre, London WC2E 9AN

T: 071–379 7383

F: NIL
NF: 150 (90)   . . .
[6, 7, 8]

Non-fiction: Editorial Director

Pitman has long been famous for its shorthand and secretarial books. Today, though, it is part of the Longman Group and specialises in more senior level books on business studies, management, computing and other technical subjects.

Pitman non-fiction books are strong on sales and marketing, accountancy, management techniques, law and banking, and information technology. Many titles are examination-oriented. Recent publications in the major areas include *How to Win Customers* by Jacques Horovitz, *Personnel Management for the Single European Market* by Mark Pinder, *Computer Security: An Integrated Approach* by Stephen Marsh and *The Management of Aviation Security* by Denis Phipps. Their titles are all very practical; geared to the needs of the studious professional as well as the professional student.

If you know a lot about a suitable, and relevant, subject, they will welcome book ideas and proposals. Pitman books should not normally be less than 180 pages long. They are seldom overwhelmed with large numbers of book proposals; in common with other technical publishers they often have to seek out and commission new, and specialist, authors.

Initial approach: detailed synopsis of non-fiction book project, accompanied by an assessment of the need and likely market for the book and a note of any competitive books; also author's credentials and a couple of sample chapters.
Decisions: within a month.
Terms: 10% of net receipts; advances go to a maximum of £500 per book.

PLUTO PRESS
(including JOURNEYMAN)

F: NIL	
NF: 45 (32)	280
[1, 7, 8, fem.]	

345 Archway Road, London N6 5AA

T: 081–348 2724

Non-fiction: Anne Beech (Editorial Director)

Pluto Press is a small but expanding publishing house which covers a broad range of opinions and debate on the Left. Founded in 1969, Pluto was bought by Zwan Publications in 1987; it then absorbed The Journeyman Press in 1989. It is going into the 1990s with a much strengthened list.

The Pluto list, exclusively non-fiction (yet they still receive the occasional unsolicited first novel!), covers philosophy, politics, and economics; women's studies, cultural studies, Irish studies, environmental, Third World, and development studies; and sociology. Pluto is primarily an academic publisher and their books reflect their scholarly approach to all subjects. Typical recent titles include *Political Theory and Animal Rights* by Clarke and Linzey, *The Socialist Debate* by Bogdan Denitch, and *Pornography, Feminism and the Individual* by Alison Assiter.

Pluto's Journeyman imprint has several fiction titles in the backlist — notably Jack London's classic socialist novels, such as *The Iron Heel* — but no new fiction will be published. Journeyman publishes "trade" books — ie of general bookshop interest — rather than academic titles. Typical recent non-fiction titles include *English Gardens: a Political and Social History* by Martin Hoyles, and *The Blue Plaque Guide* (in association with English Heritage).

Pluto are always interested in seeing proposals for new non-fiction books. Publisher Roger van Zwanenberg says, "We are looking for authors dealing with critical subjects of the day and working in an international context. Titles which will appeal not only to British socialists, but also to politically aware people in the USA, Canada and elsewhere will be preferred." They are particularly interested in strengthening their Third World and Development Studies list; they would encourage authors who take an alternative approach to development theory.

Initial approach: for non-fiction only — a detailed synopsis, a statement of the book's objectives, the author's credentials, and ideally, two sample chapters.
Decisions: can take three months — this is a small publisher with a small staff.
Terms: royalties of 10% hb and 7.5% pb on list price. Advances are not paid.

PUFFIN BOOKS (and Viking Children's Books)

Children's F/NF	
200 (14)	1600

Part of the Penguin Group
27 Wrights Lane, London W8 5TZ

T: 071–938 2200

All, picture books, fiction and non-fiction, Puffin or Viking: *through* Publishing Director, Viking Children's Books

Puffin is the oldest, and perhaps the best-known, children's paperback imprint. Like Penguin, Puffin is almost an institution. The very first Puffin book was the original *Worzel Gummidge* — and it came out in 1941. Like most paperback houses, Puffin is basically a reprinting publisher and accepts little original material, which should be sent to Viking Children's books. Viking Children's books is the children's hardback imprint of Penguin Books. Many Viking Children's books later appear in Puffin; Puffin also takes books from hardback publishers other than Viking.

Viking Children's Books cover the full range of children's books: from picture books, through first "read-alone" books, and books for 8–12 year olds and on to books for young teenagers. The Viking backlist includes many well-known titles such as *Stig of the Dump* by Clive King, Jill Murphy's *The Worst Witch*, and reprints of J. M. Barrie's *Peter Pan* and Kenneth Graham's *The Wind in the Willows*. And there are a number of books by such well-known children's writers as Dick King-Smith and Jan Mark.

More recent Viking titles include a reissue of Rosemary (no relation) Wells's picture book *Benjamin and Tulip*, the prolific Tony Bradman's *Gerbil Crazy*, Frank Rodgers' *The Intergalactic Kitchen* (a mix of text and comic-strip), and *The Great Smile Robbery* by Roger McGough. For teenagers, recent titles in the Kestrel series include *So Long at the Fair* and several books of short stories including one of 13 teenage love stories from Australia, edited by P. E. Matthews, called *State of the Heart*. Viking publish only a small amount of children's non-fiction.

But they do publish some children's poetry.

Puffin Books contain many of the Viking Children titles, plus a lot more. Top contemporary Puffin writers not published by Viking include Jill Paton Walsh (*Butty Boy*, etc.) and Gene Kemp (*Charlie Lewis Plays for Time*, etc.) And of course, there is lots of Roald Dahl, and the science fiction/fantasy of John Christopher (*The Tripods*).

Initial approach: either the complete manuscript or the first few chapters — to Viking Children's Books, as above.
Decisions: usually within four to six weeks.
Terms: royalties 10% hb, 7.5% pb on home sales; advances variable.

QUARTET BOOKS LTD

Part of Namara Group
27/29 Goodge Street, London W1P 1FD

T: 071–636 3992

F: 30 (5)	250
[L, G]	
NF: 45 (10)	350

Fiction and non-fiction: Eliza Pakenham (Editorial Assistant)

Founded in 1972 by four ex-Granada employees and acquired by Naim Attallah in 1976, Quartet was originally intended — by the Granada four — to be "up-market and to the left of Penguin". Its up-market status remains; its leftward bias is not very noticeable; it is a very prestigious imprint.

The Quartet backlist includes such excellent money-spinning foundation titles as Alex Comfort's *The Joy of Sex*, Anais Nin's *Journals of a Wife*, and the partial works of Jessica Mitford and Peter Vansittart.

Among recent fiction titles are *The Wall* by Marlen Haushofer, *Pinkerton* by Franco Cordelli and *Archipelago* by Michel Rio. They have discontinued their crime list (Quartet Qrime) — no further thrillers or crime novels should be offered. (They make a plea for no science fiction, no "cheap romance", no porn, and no poetry. And they add, "If you think you are the new Jeffrey Archer or Jackie Collins — please do not approach Quartet with your work.")

Their "Quartet Encounters" series of trade paperbacks concentrates on European literature in translation. No scope here for beginners.

The list overall is slightly larger in non-fiction than in fiction with a bias towards "seriously popular" titles. Recent titles include Tom Driberg's *Ruling Passions* and *Singular Encounters* by the owner himself, Naim Attallah. They also publish a small number of — usually commissioned — jazz-related books such as *Bird Lives!* by Ross Russell, and the recent *Klook: The Story of Kenny Clarke* by Mike Hennessey.

Quartet are happy to see new book ideas — so long as they are well-presented and preferably word-processed. On the fiction side they much prefer submissions through an agent. They publish no new poetry.

Initial approach: fiction, preferably, through an agent; non-fiction, a detailed synopsis plus the "usual" assessment of need, market and competition, and author's credentials, but initially without sample chapters.
Decisions: can take three months but often less.
Terms: Quartet pay the "standard" royalties of 10% hardback and 7.5% paperback on home sales at published price; advances vary according to assessment of the book's potential.

RANDOM CENTURY CHILDREN'S BOOKS

Div of The Random Century Group

F: 60 (5)   . . .
[K all ages]
NF: 10 (2)   . . .
[all children]

Random Century House,
20 Vauxhall Bridge Road,
London SW1V 2SA

T: 071–973 9750

All: Children's Editorial Department

Random Century Children's Books brings together the children's books departments of Hutchinson, Jonathan Cape and The Bodley Head, each of whom continue to issue books under their own names.

The Jonathan Cape children's list is small but good, and almost exclusively fiction, including books by such well-known authors as Joan Aiken, William Mayne and Roald Dahl. The list is particularly strong in its picture books among which those of Quentin Blake, and ex-*Guardian* cartoonist Posy Simmonds stand out. Posy's most recent title is *The Chocolate Wedding*.

The Bodley Head children's list, too, is mainly fiction: there are picture books, books for those just starting to read alone, books for 8 to 12-year-old readers and books for teenagers. Recent picture books include *Tiger Trek* by Ted Lewin and — more indicative of the readership level — *Going to Playschool* by Sarah Garland. Among recent stories for the beginning readers are Jill Paton Walsh's *Can I Play × 4* (four linked stories); for the 8–12s recent titles have included *A New Magic* by Jean Morris and *Sniper* by Theodore Taylor. Teenage stories include *A Can of Worms* by Jan Mark and *Play Nimrod for him* by Jean Ure.

Hutchinson Children's Books cover much the same range as The Bodley Head. Typical recent titles include: picture books — *Greedyguts* by Martina Selway; 6–8s — *Mr Parker's Autumn Term* by Nick Warburton; 8–12s — *J. B. Crimebuster* by Jo Dane. Hutchinson publish slightly more children's non-fiction than the other parts of Random Century Children's — and also the occasional book of poetry for children.

And, late news: Julia MacRae Books (ex Walker Books) will be a Random Century Children's Books imprint from Spring of 1991. The new paperback imprint, Red Fox, is also part of RCCB.

Initial approach: a brief letter, outlining the synopsis of a proposed children's book is usually the best approach — other than through an agent, which is preferred.
Decisions: usually within a month.
Terms: usually 10%/7.5% hb/pb royalties on home sales list prices; no information on the size of possible advances.

93

RIVELIN GRAPHEME PRESS | Poetry: 3 (?)   ... |

The Annex, Kennet House,
19 High Street,
Hungerford, Berks RG17 0NL

T: 0488 83480

Poetry: Snowdon Barnett

A small independent publishing house founded in 1984, Rivelin Grapheme (a subsidiary of Grapheme Ltd) publishes poetry only. (That said, they have published one novel — but this was a "one-off".)

Among the poets who have been published by Rivelin Grapheme are Peter Redgrove (*The Mudlark Poems*) and Jim Burns (*Out of the Past*).

The small number of poetry publishing houses — and the large number of hopeful poets — means that the competition for publication is always fierce. Rivelin Grapheme receive about five hundred unsolicited poetry submissions each year; their total publishing expectation is under one per cent of this. Moral, don't hold your breath.

Initial approach: complete manuscripts only, directly from the poet, not through agents.
Decisions: can take as long as three months.
Terms: no payments at all; the poet is given copies of the published book to sell for himself (or herself) — and keeps 35% of the proceeds.

ROBSON BOOKS LTD

5–6 Clipstone Street, London W1P 7EB

T: 071–323 1223

F: 3 (0)	40
[L, G]	P
NF: 67 (27)	500
[1, 2, 3, 5]	H

Fiction and non-fiction: Louise Dixon (Editor)

Founded in 1973, Robson is a middling-sized general publisher whose list is strongest in popular (often show-biz) biographies and humorous books. But they also publish general non-fiction and a (very) little fiction.

Recent humour titles have included Alan Coren's *More Like Old Times*, Les Dawson's *Come Back With The Wind* and Maureen Lipman's *Thank You for Having Me*. On the biography side, recent titles include *Candidly Caine: Everything Not Many People Know About Michael Caine* by Elaine Gallagher, *The* Real *Barry Humphries* by Peter Coleman, and *Secrets of The Royals* by Gordon Winter and Wendy Kochman. Throughout, big "names" dominate the unashamedly popular list.

The general non-fiction list too has its share of names, with Harry Secombe's *Second Highway Companion* and Gyles Brandreth's *The Word Book*. There is also *Drama in the Air* John Beattie and *Not With My You Husband Don't!* by Margaret Kent. Robson writers tend to stick with Robson — and produce new books with some regularity. There are sports books too, including recently, *Barry McGuigan: The Untold Story* by Barry McGuigan, and *Test of Fire* by Graham Gooch. There is a strong music list too, which includes *Music Sounded Out* by Alfred Brendel and *The Music Lover's Literary Companion* by Dannie and Joan Abse.

Initial approach: fiction— the first few chapters plus a synopsis — but don't hold your breath, they are very much non-fiction oriented; non-fiction — a preliminary letter, outlining the proposed book, and be ready to follow up with synopsis etc. As ever, you will have most chance of success if you are already a household name.
Decisions: can take up to three months.
Terms: royalties on home sales are the "standard" 10%/7.5% hardback/-paperback, paid twice yearly; advances vary widely.

SALAMANDER BOOKS LTD

129–137 York Way, London N7 9LG

T: 071–267 4447

F: NIL
NF: 70 (7)   . . .
[2, 3, 4, 5]

Non-fiction: Ray Bonds (Managing Director)

Salamander, which was founded in 1973, is an exclusively non-fiction house. Overall, the Salamander list contains hundreds of books on "hardware" for the armed forces (land, air and sea), and personalities, pets and petcare, cookery, crafts and gardening.

The military list includes illustrated reviews of weapons, vehicles, boats and airplanes, all of past, present and future; if you can produce a total coverage of the bow and arrow or of some futuristic ray-gun, it might well be worth approaching Salamander. Recent titles range from Bill Gunston's *Combat Arms: Modern Helicopters* through *Aces Past* by Lindsay Peacock and Patrick Bunce, to *Naval Firepower* by Lindsay Peacock. (Lindsay Peacock is a prolific Salamander author — there are several more titles by him in the new releases.)

Within their various non-military lists they have a number of ongoing series, including: *The Creative Book of* . . . (already, *Flowercraft, Gift Wrapping, Stencilling Designs*, and others); *A Gourmet's Book of* . . . (already, *Dried Fruit and Nuts, Mushrooms and Truffles*, and *Shellfish*), and *The Miniature Book of* . . . (*Dried Flowers, Flower Arranging, Napkin Folding, Gift Wrapping* and *Pot Pourri*, to name but a few).

There are also many other books, not quite so series-linked, but all very practical, encyclopaedic, and/or "how to"; recent titles include *A Discovery Guide: Rocks and Minerals* by Chris Pellant, *Captivating Cats* by Marc and Fiona Henrie, *Water in the Garden* by James Allison, *The Wines of the America* by Robert Joseph, and *The Masters of Showjumping* by Ann Martin.

They say, "Concepts must be very original and highly graphic in content, and suitable for major international markets." Their books are republished in a variety of languages.

Initial approach: detailed synopsis plus assessment of need and market, and the author's credentials; sample chapters are not required initially. Do study one or two Salamander books before submitting a proposal — they have their own unique style.
Decisions: may take as long as three months.
Terms: they do not pay royalties at all; they purchase manuscripts outright.

SECKER & WARBURG

Subsidiary of Octopus Publishing Group
Michelin House
81 Fulham Road, London SW3 6RB

T: 071–581 9393

F: 30 (5)	?*
[L]	P
NF: 30 (10)	?*
[1, 2, 3, 5]	
	*Total 480

Fiction and non-fiction: The Editorial Department
Poetry: Robin Robertson

Founded in 1910, "reconstructed" in 1936 (when Warburg joined Secker), and taken over, with Heinemann, by Octopus in 1987, Secker & Warburg are very literary publishers. They have some very fine — albeit rather "highbrow" — names among their past authors: George Orwell, Franz Kafka, and Colette, to name just three.

They themselves classify their fiction list as "literary" — which is, of course, a "moveable feast" — but it includes a wide range of writers. Current top writers range from Academic Man's favourite crime writer, Umberto Eco — of *The Name of the Rose* fame — through humorists Tom Sharpe (*Wilt*, etc.) and David Lodge, to Gunter Grass and Saul Bellow. A recent title which aroused great interest was Piers Paul Read's *On the Third Day*.

Their non-fiction list, as typified by recent books, is also somewhat heavy. Among many titles there are *Sons of the Yellow Emperor: The Story of the Overseas Chinese* by Lynn Pan, *Thomas Cook: 150 Years of Popular Tourism* by Piers Brendon, and *Lipstick Traces: A Secret History of the Twentieth Century* by Greil Marcus. They do not have any particular well-defined and expanding series into which new non-fiction titles can be steered.

Secker & Warburg are major publishers of poetry and are always willing to consider new writers. Virtually all of their poetry is published in slim, 64-page paperbacks.

Initial approach: for both fiction and non-fiction — and for poetry too — Secker & Warburg ask for a written query first, outlining what is on offer.
Decisions: up to three months.
Terms: royalties 10% hb/7.5% pb on list price home sales; 10% of net receipts on overseas sales; advances vary with a book's assessed potential.

SEREN BOOKS

The imprint of Poetry Wales Press Ltd
Andmar House, Tondu Road,
Bridgend, Mid Glamorgan CF31 4LJ

T: 0656 767834

F: 1–2 (1–2)	10
[L]	P
Poetry: 9 (1)	56
NF: 10 (8)	20
[1, 7]	

Fiction and non-fiction: Mick Felton (Editor)
Poetry: Amy Wack (Poetry Editor)

A small, but growing, publisher once predominantly of poetry but now increasingly diversifying, Seren Books was founded in 1981 — in a back bedroom — as Poetry Wales Press. (The name *Seren* is Welsh for star.) They are now looking for drama (plays by established authors only), critical books, biographies and some fiction — all with some Welsh connection — and of course, for poetry. They are now slightly less insistent on all their poets having a Welsh background.

(They also publish a quarterly magazine *Poetry Wales* which has just celebrated its 25th anniversary.)

Among the poets in their list are: Jean Earle, with *Selected Poems*, Mike Jenkins, with *A Dissident Voice*, and fellow Allison & Busby author Peter Finch with *Selected Poems*. Recent drama titles include *The View from Row G* by Dannie Abse and three plays by Gwyn Thomas.

Seren have recently launched two series of biographies: "Welsh Lives" and "Border Lines". A recent title in the Welsh series is Peter Stead's *Richard Burton: So Much, So Little*; the "Border Lines" series concentrates on writers, artists and musicians with links to the Welsh/English border counties. One early title in the Border series is Gladys Mary Coles' *Mary Webb*. (Mary Webb is a much-neglected Shropshire author — of, for example, *Precious Bane* — who won the 1924 Prix Femina.)

Their small fiction list includes Caradoc Evans' *My People* — which was in trouble when first published, for its outspoken attack on the "chapel dictators". Seren also publish a posthumous collection of the short stories of Alun Lewis. Newer fiction comes from the pens of such as Chris Meredith and Leslie Norris.

Initial approach: fiction and poetry — submit the full manuscript (or collection of poems). Non-fiction — submit the customary synopsis, assessment of market, and author's credentials — and have sample chapters ready waiting. Overall, obviously, anything with a pronounced Welsh emphasis will have the best chance.

Decisions: usually within a month.

Terms: royalties of 10% on list price of both hb and pb sales. Advances are negotiable.

SERPENT'S TAIL

4 Blackstock Mews, London N4 2BT

T: 071–354 1949

F: 25 (5)   100
[L, C]
NF: 3 (3)
[1, 2]

Fiction and non-fiction: Peter Ayrton

Serpent's Tail was founded in 1986 with the intention of publishing "non-mainstream" literary books from all over the world. By late 1990 they had a list of just under a hundred titles, around 90% of which are fiction.

You can quickly get a good "feel" for the type of books published by Serpent's Tail by a glance through their list. This includes such books as Capital Gay Book of the Year *Who Was That Man?* which is a meditative biography of Oscar Wilde by Neil Bartlett, and a translation of Elfriede Jelinek's evocative novel of life in post-war Austria *Wonderful, Wonderful Times*.

Of more interest to the new writer are two new series. Under the title *The 90s* Serpent's Tail are publishing high quality books by new writers from anywhere in the English-speaking world. One recent book in this series is *Darker Days than Usual*, a first novella plus several short stories from Suzannah Dunn — a graduate of The University of East Anglia's creative writing course. Another *90s* title is the witty *Nudists May be Encountered* by Londoner Mary Scott.

The other new Serpent's Tail series is called *Mask Noir* and consists of pacey but literary thrillers. Typical titles here include a translation (from the Spanish) of Manuel Montalban's *The Angst-Ridden Executive* and New York psychoanalyst Elsa Lewin's *I, Anna*. *I, Anna* is "a passion-hate tale of a desperate woman, a lonely detective, and a victim who demanded more than Anna could offer."

Most non-fiction books in the Serpent's Tail list relate to the world of music, and "popular culture". You need to be in this world to write about it. Serpent's Tail receive around 300 unsolicited manuscripts a year — and more than 80% are quite unsuitable, often because they are not relevant.

Initial approach: Serpent's Tail prefer an initial written enquiry, to sound out their interest, and then, if encouraged, followed by a sample chapter and a synopsis. They are actively seeking new books for their *90s* series and, maybe, for the *Mask Noir* series.

Decisions: usually about six weeks.

Terms: basically 7.5% of list price on original paperbacks and an advance of perhaps £1,000.

SEVERN HOUSE PUBLISHERS LTD

35 Manor Road,
Wallington, Surrey SM6 0BW

T: 081–773 4161

F: 120 (25)   320
[G, C, W, R, S]
NF: NIL

Fiction: Joan Simpson (or *via agent* to Edwin Buckhalter)

Founded in 1974, Severn House has built up a strong list of determinedly popular fiction — the mainstay of many a public library. In all, the current stocklist contains over 300 titles. Their always small non-fiction list is being abandoned.

The fiction list is, of course, particularly strong in *genre* titles: romances, crime/mystery/suspense, and science fiction/horror. Glancing through the list of authors there are books by such familiar names as Barbara Cartland, Jennifer Wilde, Alan Dean Foster and Piers Anthony. Apart from the *genre* lists, Severn House also publish tie-ins with TV and films.

A recent romance fiction list includes Marion Chesney's *At The Sign of the Golden Pineapple*, and *Blackmaddie*, by fellow Allison & Busby author Jean Saunders, under her pen-name of Rowena Summers. And another one by Barbara Cartland. On the crime/mystery side there is Margaret Yorke's *Mortal Remains*.

Severn House receive about 300 fiction manuscripts per year — but they *much* prefer them to come in through an agent. Agents know just what Severn House wants; their chosen area of operation — the hardcover library market — is very specific. In a recent 12-month period, they only accepted one unsolicited un-agented novel.

They say, "If it's not good enough for an agent, it's probably not good enough for a publisher either."

Initial approach: for fiction preferably through an agent; if not, send them a letter with a detailed synopsis and details of the author's credentials.
Decisions: can take as long as three months.
Terms: royalties 10% on hardback list price sales, paid twice-yearly. Advances are negotiable, varying from book to book and author to author.

SHELDON PRESS

An imprint of The SPCK (The Society
for Promoting Christian Knowledge)
SPCK Building
Marylebone Road, London NW1 4DU

T: 071–387 5282

F: NIL
NF: 30 (20)   120
[4, 6]

Non-fiction: Judith Longman (Editorial Director)
            Joanna Moriarty (Senior Editor)

Sheldon Press is a "middling-small" publisher specialising in non-fiction
self-help books about health and popular medicine, and self-develop-
ment — not only in specific management situations but also in "the world
in general". Virtually all new books published by Sheldon come within
their series "Overcoming Common Problems".

A good idea of the types of books in the series can be obtained from
a look at the titles of current books. Among recent books are: *Your
Grandchild and You*, the third successful Sheldon title by Rosemary
Wells (no relation), *How to be a Successful Secretary* by Sue Dyson and
Stephen Hoare, *Slay Your Own Dragons* by Dr Nancy Good, *How to
Study Successfully* by Michele Brown, and *Helping Children Cope with
Stress* by Ursula Markham. There is also the best-selling *Body Language*
by Allan Pease, and a whole variety of books about specific ailments —
from alcoholism to arthritis, from bowel irritation to thrush to tinnitus,
from depression to hysterectomy — and several about conquering shy-
ness.

Sheldon Press welcome non-fiction "how to" book proposals within
their areas of interest.

Initial approach: non-fiction only, provide a detailed synopis for the
proposed book, an assessment of who the book is meant for (ie the
market) and why there is a need for it, the author's credentials and, but
not necessarily initially, a couple of sample chapters.
Decisions: up to two months, but usually quicker.
Terms: royalties of 10% on hardback list price and 7.5% rising to 10%
on paperback price are paid on home sales. (Some of their titles are
published simultaneously in hardback and paperback but most are in
paperback only.) Advances vary with the book's potential.

SIDGWICK & JACKSON LTD

Division of Pan/Macmillan Ltd
18–21 Cavaye Place, London SW10 9PG
T: 071–373 6070

F: 5 (2)	45
[G, C, R]	
NF: 50 (1)	300
[1, 3, 4, 5, 6]	H

Fiction and non-fiction: Susan Hill (Editorial Director)

Sidgwick & Jackson were founded in 1908; in 1986 they were bought by Macmillan, under whose wing they still remain. Their backlist contains around four hundred books, of which the fiction element is currently only about five per cent. They are very much a non-fiction house — and a very glossy, upmarket one too.

The non-fiction list covers history, current affairs, business management, biographies and memoirs, showbiz books, and "the rest". Among the many big names who write for Sidgwick & Jackson is Shirley Conran, with the so-appropriately titled *Superwoman*. They also published Sir John Hackett's book *The Third World War*.

Another well-known name in the Sidgwick & Jackson list is Chapman Pincher; a recent book of his is *The Truth about Dirty Tricks: From Harold Wilson to Margaret Thatcher*. Other recent titles, demonstrating the spread of the list and the calibre of the "names", include *The Women Who Won the War* by Vera Lynn with Robin Cross and Jenny de Gex, *The Triads* by investigative reporter David Black, Patrick Moore's *Yearbook of Astronomy*, *Game Plan: An Independent Woman's Survival Kit* by sex-symbol Kate O'Mara, and *Mightier Than the Sword: A Study of Japanese Economic Imperialism* by Michael Heseltine.

Their backlist also includes management books by guru Robert Heller — and the most famous of them all, *Parkinson's Law* by C. N. Parkinson.

Sidgwick & Jackson are strong on showbiz books. Recent titles include *The Other Side of Lennon* by Sandra Shevey and *The Quiet One: A Life of George Harrison* by Alan Clayson. There are also recent books about the Sex Pistols, Queen, and the Pet Shop Boys.

Sidgwicks receive about five hundred non-fiction book proposals a year; they take about 1%.

Initial approach: fiction — complete manuscript (but note how few novels they publish); non-fiction — synopsis, book and author justification and sample chapters. They also commission books from their own ideas.
Decisions: usually within six weeks.
Terms: either 10%/7.5% hardback/paperback royalty on list price UK sales, or 10% of net receipts. (And I know what I'd argue for!) Advances are generous — they can be £2,000 for novels and £4,000 for non-fiction books.

SIMON & SCHUSTER LTD

West Garden Place,
Kendal Street, London W2 2AQ

T: 071–724 7577

F: 25 (5)	85
[G, C]	
NF: 50 (40)	175
[1, 2, 3, 5]	

Fiction and non-fiction: Editorial Department

Simon & Schuster, a very large US publisher owned by Paramount, opened a British office in 1986; they are now successfully established here. They have a broad general list of fiction and non-fiction — divided approximately one-third, two-thirds.

Recent non-fiction titles include *In the Arena: A Memoir of Victory, Defeat and Renewal* by Richard Nixon, *The Good, The Bad and The Bubbly: George Best — The Autobiography*, *The Sun Also Sets: Why Japan Will Not Be Number One* by Bill Emmott, and the best-selling *Maiden* by Tracy Edwards and Tim Madge. The list also includes various travel book series, notably the Frommer Guides. A good general spread.

The fiction list ranges from best-selling novelist Virginia Andrews' *Dawn* to the more "literary" *The Antique Collector* by Glynn Hughes (shortlisted for the Whitbread award). *Genre* novels include thrillers such as Tim Sebastian's *Saviour's Gate* and John Hands' *Perestroika Christi*, the horror story *Bad Dreams* by Kim Newman, and Brian Stableford's *The Werewolves of London*. Again, a good mix.

Simon & Schuster now have a major children's list too — they bought the Macdonald Children's Book list early in 1989 — see separate report, Simon & Schuster Young Books, page 174.

Initial approach:
Decisions: no information forthcoming.
Terms:

SIMON & SCHUSTER
YOUNG BOOKS

Wolsey House, Wolsey Road,
Hemel Hempstead, Herts HP2 4SS

T: 0442 231900

F: 50 (7)	240
[K]	P
NF: 70 (18)	300
[all children's]	

All: The Publisher

Simon & Schuster Young Books include a full range of children's books, from board books, through picture books to fiction for twelve-year-olds, and general non-fiction.

Recent picture books include such titles as *A Scary Story Night* by Rob Lewis (for 3-year-olds), and *Nancy Nutall and the Mongrel* by Catherine Cookson. Recent fiction titles for 6–8-year-olds include Leon Garfield's *Fair's Fair*, Frieda Hughes' *Waldorf and the Sleeping Granny* and Keith Brumpton's *Peeping Duck Gang* stories. For slightly older children, 9+, there are such titles as the *Drina* books by Jean Estoril (one such is *Drina Ballerina*), Tom Tully's *Robbo* books, including *Robbo 2, The World 0*, and Katherine Hersom's *The Half Child*. Much of the children's fiction — for all age groups — tends to fit into series.

Children's non-fiction titles also generally fit into series. Series titles include "Women History Makers", "Inside Story" and "Save our World". All the books in most of these series are 48 pages long; all are heavily illustrated. Careful market study would be needed before offering a non-fiction book to any of the Simon & Schuster children's series. (So what's new?)

The Publisher comments, wisely and helpfully: "Authors should not assume when researching publishers' lists that they/we always look for more of the same. This is particularly true of children's books. There is only room for a limited number of books on, for example, Countries, Ballet, etc. in the marketplace. Similarly, a 'gap' in the market may be a 'gap' in demand; reasons for publishing in an overcrowded market need to be precise and well-researched."

Initial approach: fiction — preferably through an agent; if direct, only the first few chapters plus a synopsis of the rest. For non-fiction, the usual detailed synopsis, assessment of need and market (and remember the detailed advice above), author's credentials and two sample chapters.
Decisions: can take three months.
Terms: Simon & Schuster Young Books prefer not to disclose details of their royalty terms or advances which vary with the type of book, the illustrative content, and various other factors.

SOUVENIR PRESS LTD

43 Great Russell Street,
London WC1B 3PA

T: 071–580 9307

F: 10 (3)	200
[L, G, C, S, R]	
NF: 45 (35)	400
[1–6 incl]	H

Fiction and non-fiction: Tessa Harrow (Editor-in-Chief)

Founded in 1952 by Ernest Hecht and still totally independent, Souvenir Press has a backlist of about 600 books divided approximately one-third fiction, two-thirds non-fiction.

Among the big-name fiction writers in the Souvenir list are Arthur Hailey (*Airport*, *Hotel*, etc.) and Peter O'Donnell (all the *Modesty Blaise* books). The non-fiction list too has several "names": the well-known management text *The Peter Principle*, by Laurence Peter and Raymond Hull is there, as is Erich von Daniken's *Chariot of the Gods*. Elsewhere, the non-fiction list includes books on cricket by Neville Cardus, on music by Gerard Hoffnung, on gardening by Alan Titchmarsh and, for children, Althea's *Brightstart* books.

Recent fiction titles include Keith Barnard's terrifying *Embryo* and Frances Paige's *The Sholtie Flyer*.

Non-fiction titles recently issued range from *A Cat is Watching: A Look at the Way Cats See Us* by Roger A. Caras, through *The Legend that is Buddy Holly* by Richard Peters and *Self-Help for Your Anxiety* by Robert Sharpe, to *Fans* by Nancy Armstrong.

They also have a series of true stories of spectacular crimes. One recent title is *The Pimlico Murder: The Strange Case of Adelaide Bartlett* by Kate Clarke.

Another part of the non-fiction list is their much-praised "Human Horizons" series for the disabled and for those who care for them. This has some sixty titles including, recently, *Gardening is for Everyone: A Week-by-week Guide for People with Handicaps* by Audrey Cloet and Chris Underhill.

Initial approach: for both fiction and non-fiction, they prefer a written enquiry, briefly outlining the proposal. Don't send them a manuscript unless and until they ask; but they welcome suggestions.
Decisions: up to three months.
Terms: royalties are 10% hb, 7.5% pb on list price home sales; advances vary, depending on potential.

SPHERE BOOKS
(incl. ABACUS & CARDINAL)

Division of Macdonald & Co (Publ) Ltd
(Member of Maxwell Macmillan
Pergamon Publishing Corporation PLC)
Orbit House, 1 New Fetter Lane,
London EC4A 1AR

T: 071–377 4600

F: 100 (10)	950
[G, C, S]	
NF: 70 (50)	750
[1, 3, 6]	H

All fiction and non-fiction: Barbara Boote (Publishing Director)

Founded in 1967 and for a brief while, part of the Penguin group, Sphere is a mass-market paperback publisher, now an imprint of Macdonald & Co (*see* page 109). Their list is huge and growing steadily. (They are offered nearly 2,000 manuscripts a year; only about 10% are accepted.)

Many favourite authors are with Sphere: Danielle Steel inevitably takes pride of place, but with Emma Blair, Janet Dailey and Judith Michael hard on her heels — all with stories beloved of women readers. Sphere is big in SF and fantasy too with such top authors as Larry Niven (*Ringworld*) and, together with Jerry Pournelle, *Footfall*. Sphere has Harry Harrison's delightful *Stainless Steel Rat* stories and Gordon R. Dickson's *Dorsai* series. Recent more general Sphere titles include Claire Rayner's *Flapper* and Stephen King's *Dark Tower II: The Drawing of the Three*.

In non-fiction, Sphere books range from the lovely *Bizarre Books* by Russell Ash and Brian Lake, through Robert Bruce's *Winners* (about Industrial Achievement Award winners), to *79 Ways to Calm a Crying Baby* by Diana S. Greene. They have books on management too.

Sphere has two subsidiary imprints: Abacus and Cardinal. Abacus publishes around 30 fiction titles a year, mainly "literary", and a handful of non-fiction books. Among Abacus authors are Alison Lurie and Truman Capote; one recent title was Louise Erdrich's *Love Medicine*. Cardinal is a non-fiction imprint publishing mainly popular history and biography; authors include Frederick Raphael and historian E. J. Hobsbawm. One recent title was Clive Ponting's *1940: Myth & Reality*.

On the popular fiction front, Sphere are always "looking for something 'different'."

Initial approach: fiction — the first three chapters and a synopsis of the rest. Non-fiction — detailed synopsis with assessment of need, and author's credentials.
Decisions: usually within one to two months.
Terms: royalties 7.5% pb on list price; "first-timer" advances, up to £4000 for fiction and £3000 for non-fiction.

**STANLEY THORNES
(PUBLISHERS) LTD**

F: NIL
NF: 200 (0)   1800
[8]

Old Station Drive, Leckhampton,
Cheltenham, Gloucs. GL53 0DN

T: 0242 228888

Non-fiction: Jayne De Courcy (Deputy Managing Director)

A sizeable independent publisher, Stanley Thornes specialises in educational textbooks. Their coverage spreads from primary level, through
secondary and higher levels, to further education, and across virtually all
subjects — and they are interested in book ideas for anything suitable
for this market. Such books will usually, but not exclusively, be written
by current or ex-teachers, lecturers or other educators.

Typical of some of the books they publish are those by Thelma Foster.
An ex-lecturer with specialist knowledge relevant to college curricula, she
has written several books for Thornes, including *Office Skills, Building
Secretarial Competence* and *Secretarial Procedures*. Among the textbooks
specifically for GCSE are *GCSE Mathematics* by Greer and *British Economic and Social History* by Sauvain.

Initial approach: Thornes prefer a written query first, outlining the subject
and suggested treatment, to be followed up with the usual detailed synopsis, assessment of need and market, author's credentials and two sample
chapters.
Decisions: no more than three months.
Terms: royalties of 10% of net receipts are normal. Advances vary.

THORSONS PUBLISHERS

Part of HarperCollins Publishers
77–85 Fulham Palace Road,
London W6 8JB

T: 081-741 7070

F: NIL
NF: 200 (90)   2250
[1–7 incl]

Non-fiction: Eileen Campbell (Publishing Director)

Thorsons Publishers was founded in 1930; it took over Aquarian Press in 1955; it expanded further during the mid-Eighties. In 1989 it was acquired by Collins — now HarperCollins Publishers, part of News International.

Thorsons has long been recognised as a major publisher of books on alternative medicine, nutrition, self-help and positive thinking. The huge Thorsons stocklist covers a wide variety of categories: alternative therapies, astrology and astronomy, business success, public speaking, comparative religion, cookery and diets, "paths to inner power" and magic — to name just a few.

Recent titles from Thorsons include *The Green Bible* by Colin Johnson, *Eczema Relief* by Christine Orton, *Aromatherapy for Women* by Maggie Tisserand, *Sexual Power* by Sandra Sedgbeer, *No-Fault Negotiating* by Len Leritz and *A Whack on the Side of the Head* by Roger von Oech.

The Aquarian Press is a separate imprint under the Thorsons umbrella. It publishes books on the occult, astrology, magic, etc. Recent titles range from *The Celtic Tarot Pack* by Courtney Davis and Helena Paterson, through *Understanding the Chakras* (a person's 7 vital force centres) by Peter Rendel, to *The Art of Sexual Ecstasy* by Margo Anand.

As part of the reorganisation of Thorsons within HarperCollins — and the HarperCollins takeover of Unwin Hyman — Unwin's Pandora and Mandala imprints are also now under the Thorsons umbrella. Mandala is a "New Age" imprint — with titles like *Creative Astrology* by Prudence Jones and *Mahayana Buddhism* by Beatrice Lane Suzuki; Pandora is a feminist list which publishes both fiction and non-fiction (*see* page 133).

Initial approach: Thorsons welcome non-fiction book proposals — submit detailed synopsis, assessment of market, need and competition, and author's credentials. Have sample chapters ready but don't send them until asked. Overall book length not less than 40,000 words.
Decisions: can take two months if expert consultation is necessary, but can be very speedy when necessary.
Terms: usually 10% hb, 7.5% trade pb, 6% mass pb on home sales and 10% of net receipts on overseas sales. Advances vary.

VIKING BOOKS

The hardback imprint of Penguin Books
27 Wrights Lane, London W8 5TZ

T: 071–938 2200

F: 40 (4)	120
[L, G, C, S]	
NF: 50 (20)	430
[1, 2, 3, 5, 6]	

Adult fiction and non-fiction: The Publishing Director

The successor to Allen Lane, as the complement to the paperback Penguins (*see* page 137), Viking Books has taken off in a big way. It successfully publishes just under a hundred books a year, and has some excellent writers in its list. They are offered over five hundred books a year, roughly half fiction, half non-fiction; however, they publish very few first novels. But about 40% of their non-fiction books are by writers new to the list.

Recent additions to the Viking adult fiction list include six short stories by John Mortimer under the title of *Rumpole à la Carte*, Lisa Alther's new *Bedrock*, *Get Shorty* by leading US crime writer Elmore Leonard, and J. P. Donleavy's *That Darcy, That Dancer, That Gentleman*. Needless to say, all of these fiction titles will almost certainly be reissued in Penguin.

Viking non-fiction covers most areas other than the instructional or craft book and educational or academic texts. It is, again, a "popular quality" list. It also includes the Microsoft, Granta, Reinhardt, Arkana and Allen Lane imprints.

Recent non-fiction titles include biographies such as *Pet Shop Boys, Literally* by Chris Heath, *The Sun in the Morning*, the autobiography of M. M. Kaye (author of *The Far Pavilions*), *The Virgin Queen* by Christopher Hibbert and *The Invisible Woman: The Story of Nelly Ternan and Charles Dickens* by Claire Tomalin. More general Viking non-fiction includes *The Land Within the Passes: A History of Xi'an* by Zou Zongxu and *The Penguin Book of Lies* edited by Philip Kerr. In the smaller imprints there are such recent titles as *The Vikings* by Else Roesdahl (Allen Lane), *Secrets of the Soil* by Peter Tompkins and Christopher Bird (Arkana), and *The Last Word — and other stories* by Graham Greene (Reinhardt).

Poetry is only considered from "established poets".

Initial approach: fiction, either complete manuscript or the first few chapters and a synopsis; non-fiction, detailed synopsis, assessment of need, market and competition, and author's credentials — but no sample chapters.
Decisions: usually within six weeks.
Terms: usually 10% hb, 7.5% pb on list price home sales. Advances vary.

VIRAGO PRESS LTD

Centro House,
20/23 Mandela Street,
London NW1 0HQ

T: 071–383 5150

F: 75 (3) . . .
[L, G, C, K]   P
NF: 35 (16) . . .
[1, 2, 3, 4, 5, 7
& feminist]

Fiction and non-fiction: Lennie Goodings (Editorial Director)
Virago Modern Classics: Alexandra Pringle (Editorial Director)

Founded in 1972 by Carmen Callil as a publisher of books by, for, and about women, Virago quickly established a place for itself and its glossy green-covered paperbacks. From the start, it published both reprints of books by women writers of the past, and present-day originals. In the mid-Eighties, Virago was part of a larger publishing group, but it is now once again an independent company — still headed up by Carmen Callil.

The Virago fiction list is in three broad sections — their "Classics" and "Modern Classics" (reprints of novels by women); their new fiction list; and their "Virago Upstarts", ("wicked, wise and witty" books — fiction and non-fiction — for teenagers and young women). They also have a fast-growing Virago Crime series.

Recent titles in the new general fiction list include Ann Oakley's second novel, *Matilda's Mistake*, Ellen Galford's *Queendom Come*, and Japanese actress and politician Chinatsu Nakayama's *Behind the Waterfall* (translated by Geraldine Harcourt). Ann Oakley's first novel *The Men's Room* (Virago) is being serialised on TV.

The Crime series has recently been enhanced by the addition of such titles as the American Amanda Cross's latest, *The Theban Mysteries* and — another well-known American — Sara Paretsky's *Burn Marks*.

Recent new non-fiction titles include Australian playwright Dorothy Hewett's autobiography *Wild Card*, *Into the Darkness Laughing: The Story of Modigliani's Last Mistress, Jeanne Hebuterne* by Patrice Chaplin, and *The Catch of Hands*, Benedicta Leigh's passionate story of her sometimes eccentric, but always full life.

Virago also publish poetry. Recently they have published *I Shall Not Be Moved* by Maya Angelou, Margaret Atwood's *Poems: 1965–75*, and *the Virago Book of Love Poetry* edited by Wendy Mulford.

Initial approach: fiction — whole manuscript: non-fiction — the usual detailed synopsis plus assessment of need and market, and author's credentials.
Decisions: usually within about a month.
Terms: "industry-standard" 10% hb and 7.5% pb on home sales; advances vary with a book's potential.

VIRGIN PUBLISHING
(previously W. H. ALLEN)

(incl. W. H. Allen, Allison & Busby,
Doctor Who and
Nexus)
Part of the Virgin Group
338 Ladbroke Grove, London W10 5AH

T: 081–968 7554

F: 70 (0)   . . .
[S, erotica]
NF: 80 (. .)   . . .
[1, 3, 5 and showbiz]

Virgin/W. H. Allen: Peter Day (Editorial Director)
Doctor Who/Nexus: Peter Darvill-Evans

Founded over 150 years ago, W. H. Allen became part of Richard
Branson's Virgin Group and, early in 1991 was renamed Virgin Books.
As a result of financial problems at the old W. H. Allen, the company
was dramatically restructured during 1990: the Star paperback imprint
and the Mercury Business Books lists were shed and all general fiction
publishing was dropped. (But see too Allison & Busby — page 11 —
which is also part of the Virgin Group, and which retains a thriving
literary and popular fiction and non-fiction list including the *Writers'
Guides*.)

Most general "trade" publishing now appears under the Virgin imprint
and is concentrated in Virgin's long-standing areas of strength: film,
TV and video tie-in titles, music, travel, and showbiz biographies and
autobiographies. The W. H. Allen imprint is now reserved for titles
within its own strengths: popular science, true crime, politics, history,
militaria and other biographies. Overall, Virgin is now a lean and carefully "focused" publisher.

Recent successful Virgin (including W. H. Allen) titles include illustrated books about Motown, James Dean, and the Paparazzi; biographies
of Jane Fonda, Bette Davis and Yasser Arafat; and popular science books
such as *The Arrow of Time*, and *Too Hot to Handle: the story of the race
for cold fusion*, by Professor Frank Close.

Virgin also has two specialist mass-market paperback lists: "Doctor
Who" and "Nexus". The Doctor Who list has long consisted of TV
novelisations but it is now also commissioning original Doctor Who novels
for an adult audience. The Nexus list is solely erotic fiction. Between
them, these two lists commission and publish over 70 mass-market fiction
titles annually — and sell over a million copies between them.

Initial approach: non-fiction — detailed synopsis with appraisal of need
and market, and author's credentials; fiction (Nexus and Doctor Who) —
complete manuscript.
Decisions: usually within four to six weeks.
Terms: standard trade terms (basically 10% hb/7.5% pb on list price
home sales) on Virgin/W. H. Allen titles; "mass market royalties" on

Nexus/Doctor Who titles. Advances vary with the sales potential of the book.

WALKER BOOKS LTD

87 Vauxhall Walk, London SE11 5HJ

T: 071–793 0909

F: 370 (0) . . .
[children's]
NF: negligible

Fiction: Editorial Department

Founded by Sebastian Walker in 1979, Walker Books specialise very successfully — in children's books. They publish in both hardback and paperback, with titles ranging from picture books to young adult fiction; they put out about 350-plus new titles per year. They receive some 50 unsolicited manuscripts each week; they publish virtually no first (children's) novels at all.

They are a prestigious publisher to be with — and one that looks after its authors well. During 1990 Sebastian Walker set up a trust to which he transferred 51% of the company's shares; all employees of the company will be potential beneficiaries; all Walker authors and artists have been invited to become £100 per annum "employees" (without losing their freedom to publish with other companies) — and therefore potential beneficiaries too. Payments from the trust are entirely discretionary, but the trust can only be to the benefit of Walker authors, who will also feel more "involved" in their publisher's fortunes.

The Walker Books list is perhaps strongest in its picture books. Mostly 24 or 32 pages long with only a few very well-chosen words, these include such recent titles, picked at random, as *The Wish Factory* by Chris Riddell, *The Whistling Piglet* by Dick King-Smith and Norman Johnson, *Jolly Roger* by Colin McNaughton, and *The Grumpalump* in verse, by Sarah Hayes and illustrated by award-winning Barbara Firth.

For 7–10 year-old readers one recent title is Jill (*Worst Witch*) Murphy's hilarious tale of a knight called *Geoffrey Strangeways*. For slightly older readers, in paperback, there is Hannah Coles' recent *Kick-Off* — making a case for unisex soccer. For young adults, Geoffrey Trease has his one hundredth (!) book *The Calabrian Quest*. In paperback for young adults, another recent title was Christa Laird's *Shadow of the Wall* — a very powerful story about life in the Warsaw ghetto.

One of their very few non-fiction titles is Ian Redmond's *The Elephant Man*.

Initial approach: don't just send in a manuscript "out of the blue", write and tell them about it first — briefly. Thereafter, if interested, they will look at the first couple of chapters.
Decisions: can take three months.
Terms: "will be discussed once the manuscript has been accepted."

FRANKLIN WATTS

Divison of The Watts Group
96 Leonard Street, London EC2A 4RH

T: 071–739 2929

F: NIL
NF: 250 (20)   750
[children's interests]

Non-fiction: Ruth Taylor (Managing Editor)

Established in London in 1969, Franklin Watts is linked to the American house of the same name (which was founded in 1942). The Watts Group, including Franklin Watts and its associated imprint, Orchard Books (*see* page 126) are specialist publishers of children's books; Franklin Watts publish non-fiction, Orchard publish fiction.

All of the Franklin Watts non-fiction books are in short, usually eight-book, series; in many cases, all the books in a series are by the same author. Typical series — each with 32-page well-illustrated books — include "Science Starters" with titles including *Bouncing and Bending Light*, *Water and Life*, *Energy and Power*, all by Barbara Taylor, and "Fresh Start", with such titles (by various authors) as *Paper Crafts*, *Puppets*, *Kites*, *Christmas Crafts* and *Toy Theatres*.

For rather older child readers (11–14 age group perhaps) there are series of longer, 48-page, books such as "Hotspots", which includes *Ireland — a divided country* and *The Soviet Union — will perestroika work?*, and "Issues" with titles such as *Crack & Cocaine*, *AIDS* and *Human Rights*.

Franklin Watts welcome ideas for new books but point out that all their books are in short series; books should fit into either a 32-page or a 48-page format; they particularly recommend that potential authors familiarise themselves with their list before considering submitting. There are far too many series to adequately cover in this report; send a large (A4 size) sae for a copy of the Franklin Watts list.

Initial approach: as for adult non-fiction books, the best approach is with a detailed synopsis, an assessment of need, market and competition, and a statement of the author's credentials. It is best *not* to prepare sample chapters for children's books though — the coverage of the synopsis will often need amendment.
Decisions: quickly — within about a month at most.
Terms: an outright flat fee is offered/negotiated — royalties are *not* paid.

GEORGE WEIDENFELD & NICOLSON

91 Clapham High Street,
London SW4 7TA

T: 071–622 9933

F: 40 (10)	100
[L, G, C]	
NF: 200 (60)	700
[1, 3, 6, 7]	H

Fiction: Allegra Huston (Senior Editor — Fiction)
Non-fiction: David Roberts (Publisher — General Books)

Founded in 1949, Weidenfeld & Nicolson are "quality" non-fiction publishers. They are perhaps best-known for their histories, and biographies of everyone from Oliver Cromwell and Queen Victoria to Raisa Gorbachev and Elizabeth Taylor. But they publish much more than just memoirs. They are major art publishers, renowned for their artwork, and have a strong general list. They also publish popular management books.

Although smaller in fiction, Weidenfeld & Nicolson also have a noteworthy fiction list. The backlist includes titles by such as Vladimir Nabokov and Olivia Manning. Current fiction authors include the prolific action-thriller writer Philip McCutchan (recently, *Convoy of Fear*), Susan Crosland, witty crime-writer Neville Steed, and Claire Rayner (recently, *Blitz* — in the *Poppy Chronicles* series).

Recent general-interest non-fiction books include such titles as *Red Empire: The Forbidden History of the USSR* by Gwyneth Hughes and Simon Welfare, and *How to Take on the Media* by Sarah Dickinson. Recent illustrated books have included a history of the Greek monarchy, *The Royal House of Greece*, by Prince Michael of Greece and Alan Palmer, and the lavish *Spain* by Angus Mitchell. Many of the non-fiction subjects are topical and/or their authors well known.

Ideas for non-fiction books are welcome but it is essential that they are of really first-class quality. Weidenfeld & Nicolson receive about 1,000 non-fiction and 500 fiction book offers per year; they publish 200 and 40. Clearly, the chances are lower for fiction — but in 1990, 10 of those 40 were first novels.

Initial approach: fiction — preferably through an agent; if not, at least a query letter first. Non-fiction — provide detailed synopsis, assessment of need for the book, author's credentials, and two sample chapters.
Decisions: can take over three months, so don't hold your breath.
Terms: industry-standard royalties of 10% hb and 7.5% pb are paid on list prices. Royalties are paid six-monthly for two years after publication, and then annually. Advances can be as much as £2,000 for a first book.

THE WOMEN'S PRESS LTD

Part of Namara Group
34 Great Sutton Street,
London EC1V 0DX

T: 071–251 3007

F: 25 (12)	150
[L, G, C, S, K]	
NF: 25 (10)	150
[1, feminist]	

Fiction and non-fiction: The Editorial Director

Founded in 1978 on the rising tide of feminism, The Women's Press part of Naim Attallah's Namara Group (*see* also Quartet, page 153), is now firmly established with a list of over 300 titles in print. Their books are all feminist in attitude and are all written by women.

The Women's Press is big in original crime and publishes the only women's science fiction list. One recent crime title was Barbara Paul's *The Renewable Virgin*. In the science-fiction series, recent titles include Jane Palmer's *Moving Moosevan* and Candas Jane Dorsey's *Machine Sex . . . and Other Stories*.

The general fiction list contains many powerful stories. Typical are a book of stories by Merle Collins entitled *Rain Darling*, Christine Crow's *Miss X, or The Wolfwoman* (the story of the reciprocated passion of a schoolgirl for an older woman) and Marie Cardinal's tale of a life wrecked by a daughter's heroin addiction, *Devotion and Disorder*.

The Women's Press has a distinguished list of writing by black and Third World women, ranging from Alice Walker (*The Color Purple*) to Merle Collins (*Angel* — and see above).

They also have a "slightly dangerous" series for teenagers and young women, called "Livewire". A recent Livewire title is *Peta's Pence* by Christine Purkis — the tale of three generations of women coming to terms with the loss of Peta's brother. Earlier titles in the series included *French Letters* by Eileen Fairweather and *Push Me Pull Me*, by Sandra Chick, about the sexual abuse of children, which won The Other Award.

Non-fiction books are largely political/historical/feminist. Recent titles include *The Charge of the Parasols* (women's entry to the medical profession) by Catriona Blake and Liz Whitelaw's *The Life and Rebellious Times of Cicely Hamilton: actor, writer, suffragist*. The Women's Press Handbook series addresses practical issues; typical titles include Marilyn Lawrence's *The Anorexic Experience*.

Initial approach: fiction, preferably through an agent, but in any case, a synopsis first; they are particularly looking for scripts for "Livewires" and the Crime series. For non-fiction, a detailed synopsis, assessment of need and market, and author's credentials. Sample chapters to follow.
Decisions: within two months.
Terms: royalties usually 10% hb/7.5% pb on list price. Advances can be around £1,000.

2

Who Publishes What?

This chapter consists solely of lists: lists of the publishers and in which fields they are most interested in publishing. The lists are self-explanatory — although far from infallible — and may perhaps suggest where to look first within the detailed reports in the previous chapter.

The comparison of odds — odds on having a first novel accepted from the "slushpile" — is interesting although hardly encouraging. Without doubt, it is far easier to get a first non-fiction book accepted than a first novel.

POSSIBLE PUBLISHERS FOR YOUR FIRST NOVEL

Publisher	Novels 1990	1990 Firsts	% Firsts	Slushpile size	Slushpile chances	Worth trying
Allison & Busby	25	3	12	170	1:57	maybe
Bloomsbury Publ.	43	12	28	1000	1:83	maybe
The Bodley Head	8	4	50	550	1:138	
Jonathan Cape	50	10	20	?	?	
Carcanet Press	10	1	10	200	1:200	
Constable	30	10	33	750	1:75	maybe
André Deutsch	80	24	30	2500	1:104	maybe
Fourth Estate	15	5	33	200	1:50	yes
Victor Gollancz	167	7	4	2600	1:371	
Robert Hale	300	50	17	5000*	1:100	yes
Hamish Hamilton	40	16	40	1000	1:63	maybe
Headline Bk. Publ.	260	25	10	3000	1:120	
Lion Publishing	20	4	20	400	1:100	
Macdonald & Co	45	12	27	2000	1:167	
Macmillan London	90	6	7	250	1:42	
Malvern Publishing	6	6	100	500	1:83	yes
Mills & Boon	300	?5	1	5000	1:1000	YES!
Pandora Press	10	5	50	2000	1:400	
Paitkus Books	80	8	10	1000	1:125	
Quartet Books	30	5	17	350	1:70	maybe
Serpent's Tail	25	5	20	300	1:60	yes
Sidgwick & Jackson	5	2	40	500	1:250	
Viking Books	40	4	10	250	1:62	maybe
Virago Press	75	3	4	1400	1:350	
Weidenfeld & N'son	40	10	25	500	1:50	yes
Woman's Press	25	12	48	400	1:33	yes

Publisher	Gen'l fict	Rom	Cri	SF	West	Children F/NF (all)	Gen	How To	Spt	Man	Poe	Hum
Allison & Busby	L		o				o	o				
Angus & Robertson							o	o	o		●	
Anvil Press Poetry						o				●		
Arrow Books	o	o	o	o	o	o	o	o	o	o	●	
Bantam Press	o	o	o			o	o	o	o			
B T Batsford							o	o	o			
Blackie Children's						o						
Bloodaxe Books											o	
Bloomsbury Publ.	L		o				o	o	o	o		
The Bodley Head	L		o				o					
Business Books									o			
Cambridge U Press							Education					
Jonathan Cape	L		o	o			o				o	
Carcanet Press	L						o				o	
Cassell							o	o	o	o	●	
Century Books	o	o	o	o			o	o	o			
Chatto & Windus	L	o	o	o			o	o	o		o	
Collins Children's						o						
Collins General	L	o	o	o			o	o	o		●	
Constable	L		o				o					
Corgi	o	o	o	o	o	o	o	o	o	o	●	
David & Charles							o	o	o			
J M Dent						o	o	o	o			
Andre Deutsch	L	o	o			o	o	o	o		●	
Ebury Press							o	o				
Element Books							"New Age"					
Elliott R't Way Bks							o	o	o			
Faber & Faber	L		●			o	o	o			o	
Fontana	o	o	o	o			o			o	o	
Foulsham								o	o	o		
Fourth Estate	L						o		o		●	
Samuel French	Plays											
Futura Books	o	o	o	o	o		o	o			●	
Victor Gollancz	L		o	o		o	o	o	o			
Gower Publ. Group							Education				●	
Grafton Books	o	o	o	o		●	o		●		o	●
Robert Hale	o	o			o		o	o	o			
Hamish Hamilton	L		o			o	o	o	o			
Hamlyn Publishing							o	o	o			
Harrap							Reference					
Headline Bk. Publ.	o	o	o	o			o	o	o			o
William Heinemann	L	o	o				o		o			
Hippo Books				o		o			o		o	o
Hodder & Stoughton	L	o	o	o		o	o	o	o	o		
Hutchinson Books	o		o				o	o	o		o	
Michael Joseph	L		o				o	o	o			o
Kogan Page								o		o		
Ladybird Books						o						
Lawrence & Wishart							Socialist					
Lion Publishing	o	●	o				Religious					

NOTE: "L" indicates "literary" fiction as well as "general".

118

WHO PUBLISHES WHAT?

Publisher	Gen'l fict	Rom	Cri	SF	West	Children F/NF (all)	Gen	How To	Spt	Man	Poe	Hum
Longman Group							Education				•	
Macdonald & Co	L	o	o	o			o	o	o			o
Macmillan London	L		o				o	o	o	o		o
Malvern Publishing	L	o	o				o					
Methuen London	L		o	o			o	o				o
Mills & Boon		o										
Mitchell B'zley Int							Ref.	o	o			
New Engl. Library	o	o	o	o			o					o
Northcote H'se Publ.								o		o		
Octopus Children's						o						
Optima Books								o	o			o
Orchard Books						o					o	
Peter Owen Ltd	L						o					
Oxford Univ Press							Education				•	
Pan Books	L	o	o	o		o	o	o	o	o	o	
Pandora Press	L		•				o					
Pan/Macmillan Child's						o						
Penguin Books	L		o	o			o	o	o	o	•	
Pergamon Press							Education				•	
Peterloo Poets											o	
Phillimore & Co							Local History					
Piatkus Books	o	o	o				o	o		o		
Piccadilly Press						o						
Pitman Publishing							Technical				•	
Pluto Press							Socialist				•	
Puffin Bks (Vik Ch)						o						
Quartet Books	L						o					
Rand Cent Child's						o						
Rivelin Grapheme											o	
Robson Books	o						o					o
Salamander Books								o	o			
Secker & Warburg	L						o		o	o		
Seren Books	L						o			o		
Serpent's Tail	L		o				o					
Severn House	o	o	o	o	o							
Sheldon Press								o		o		
Sidgwick & Jackson	o	o	o				o	o	o	o		o
Simon & Schuster	o		o				o		o			
Sim & Schus Yng Bks						o						
Souvenir Press	L	o	o	o			o	o	o	o		o
Sphere Books	o		o	o			o		o			o
Stanley Thornes							Education					
Thorsons Publ.							o	o	o	o		
Viking Books	L		o	o			o		o	o		
Virago Press	L		o			o	o	o	o		o	
Virgin Books				o			o					
Walker Books						o						
Franklin Watts						o						
Weidenfeld & N'son	L		o				o		o			o
Women's Press	L		o	o		o	o					

NOTE: "L" indicates "literary" fiction as well as "general".

119

3

Advice from the Publishers

As part of the research necessary to produce each edition of this book, a questionnaire is circulated to a large number of British publishers. Among the questions, publishers are asked if they have any words of guidance or help for a new writer seeking to sell a first book. Where appropriate, the comments are incorporated in the specific reports, but some are of more general import. These are quoted below.

One of the most important points, repeated again and again by publishers, is the need for writers to study the market. Publishers are offered an awful lot of inappropriate material: even to the extent of sending manuscripts of (first) novels to exclusively non-fiction publishers — and vice versa.

As well as the need for market study, several publishers also mention the need for non-fiction authors to assess the competition. When approaching publishers, non-fiction authors should also set out clearly the purpose and content of their book.

On the fiction side, *genre* writing has a greater chance than "straight" — many publishers will welcome crime books and several have growing science-fiction and/or fantasy lists. Two leading publishers of romance fiction offer the new writer helpful tip-sheets — advice on their specific requirements, length, etc.

But generally, advice from publishers for first-time writers is:

Allison & Busby
When submitting the work the author should write initially setting out concisely the theme of the book in a clear but short synopsis. together with two sample chapters. The author should mention any previous publications, and whether or not he/she has tried to get an agent, with what results.

Cambridge University Press
Describe briefly the distinguishing features of the (non-fiction) book; say who it is for — level, subject area, countries; say who you are — academic qualifications, other publications, possible referees; take care with the presentation of the letter and the synopsis.

Constable
It should be remembered that category fiction — thrillers, historical, etc. — is much easier to sell than straight fiction. For a first novel, publisher must have a peg to hang his publicity on — contemporary issue, human drama, etc. — even just the quality of writing. Easier to sell them

non-fiction but must be a subject that reading public want to know about. Minor historical or political figures seldom sell.

Corgi
Layout of typescript very important. Double-spacing and plenty of "air" generally (to aid ease of reading). Avoid too many superlatives or hyperbole in the accompanying letter. Bracket the work as closely as possible — ie category, style, etc. — to other authors.

Fourth Estate
People trying to sell a completed book should endeavour to regard it as the business of hoping to make a bit of money out of *something already achieved*. Writing a book, even a bad one, is a considerable achievement. Don't concentrate too much on selling it — it is often frustrating. Try to go on writing.

Robert Hale
"Above all, the reader must very quickly be attracted to the story and the characters and must feel compelled to read on.

"The hero and heroine must be sympathetic characters but not 'goody-goodies' even if they are misunderstood initially." (Extract from their romance fiction tip-sheet.)

Hamish Hamilton
Be concise in any outline. If a finished script is being offered, let it be clean, tidy, well-typed and well-spaced.

Hodder & Stoughton
Read other people's books, learn about style, about how to write, from them. Be prepared to listen to advice. Don't think what you have written is necessarily saleable first time. Be humble. But above all, believe in your ability to get it right eventually — with help.

Kogan Page
Prospective authors should read our catalogues, advertisements and published reviews.

A properly prepared proposal can save an awful lot of time in getting it assessed.

Potential [non-fiction] authors should always contact an appropriate publisher *before* embarking on writing. At Kogan Page we have a very clear idea of what our markets want and how it should be presented to them.

Methuen Children's Books
For children, a strong narrative skill is essential. Please don't begin a book: "It was the first day of the summer holidays." It has been done before.

Mills & Boon
"We believe that quality is more important than quantity — that romance readers deserve the best we can find.

"We don't worry too much about flawless presentation; a book that has been written with genuine feeling can be forgiven a few typing mistakes. What is more important is a genuine love of storytelling, combined with a freshness and originality of approach. Sincerity, and belief in the characters as real people, communicate themselves to the reader . . .

"Each of our authors must possess an individual touch, her own particular way of telling a story, and this quality is vital." (Extract from their romance fiction tip-sheet.)

Northcote House
An outline and sample chapters are not enough. Authors who put forward convincing sales arguments are more likely to receive favourable consideration.

Papermac
We always appreciate a potential author showing what is on the market already, that might compete . . . because an awareness of what's around leads to less duplication . . . of ideas. We always appreciate good ideas.

Puffin (and Viking Children's Books)
We're simply looking for new and exciting work. The main advice for a new writer is to study catalogues from publishers to find out which would be most suitable to publish his/her work; and also, through libraries and bookshops, find out what is already available. It's not a bad idea to try out any writing on the target audience it's intended for (children). Get as many responses and criticisms as possible before submitting it.

Sphere
It is . . . best to obtain a literary agent rather than approach a publisher direct but, failing that, a telephone call to the publisher to obtain a contact name and initial interest is useful. Then, a covering letter with synopsis and sample two/three chapters.

Weidenfeld & Nicolson
A common mistake among would-be (non-fiction) writers is not to think through whether their good idea is in fact a *book* idea. Too often, thoughts appropriate for magazine or media documentaries etc. are presented as subjects for books, which they may well not be.

4

Presentation

Irrespective of whether you write your book manuscript by hand and then type it, or get it typed, or write directly onto a word-processor, the end result which you present to the publishers must appear the same. Small differences from the norm are unimportant but the basic presentation must be near the norm. Remember, you are seeking to *sell* your masterpiece. A good-looking MS is more likely to be looked at before — and with better grace than — one that looks a mess.

The rules of presentation are simple; they are set out below.

- The manuscript must be typed, in either *pica* or *elite* type (that is, either 10 or 12 characters to the inch).

- The MS must be typed on white A4 paper, ideally 70 or 80 gsm (the weight in grams per square metre of paper), with big margins on all four sides. You need to allow 1.5 to 2 inches (about 4.5 cm)— on the left and at least an inch (2.5 cm) on the other three sides. The typing must be double-spaced, that is, there must be a gap of a whole line (not just half a line) between each line of type.

- Each chapter of your book should start on a fresh sheet of paper. Identify the chapter number (and title, if appropriate) and then start the first paragraph a third to halfway down the page.

- Indent the start of each paragraph by a standard amount (usually 5 spaces), except the first paragraph below the chapter title or any subsequent sub-headings, which should not be indented. (Notice how any printed book is set out; opening, and similar, paragraphs are not indented.)

- Do not separate paragraphs by an extra line-space. Do, however, leave an extra line-space above and below sub-headings, which are used in non-fiction books only.

- Underline only those words which are required to be printed in *italics*; do not underline chapter titles or sub-headings.

- Number the MS pages in sequence — not by chapter (eg not pages 2/3, 2/4, 2/5 etc. in chapter 2). Number the mss pages in a standard manner — top right, or bottom right or bottom centre — and preferably in the top right corner. It helps, and is easy with a word-processor, to give a "strap" (in word-processing, a *header*) on each page, such as "Wells/63" to identify which book a stray page 63 may belong to.

- Provide drafts for the *prelims*, the standard set of pages at the front of every printed book — half-title, half-title verso, title, etc. Do not number these in sequence with the actual MS; number them i, ii, iii, etc.

- Do not staple MS pages together. Publishers will be happy to receive a box of loose, but numbered, pages; I prefer to paper-clip the pages of each chapter together. I usually fold an extra slip of rough paper over the corner too, before I clip the pages. (This makes it easier to unclip and avoids the possibility of tearing, or rust-marks on the pages.)

- Make sure that your real name, or your pen-name, is on the title page of the book MS and on the last page too. But also put your real name and address on both first and last pages too. (If providing a "strap" *see above*, use your pen-name for it.)

- Deliver the MS in a recycled paper box or, as I do, in a cardboard wallet. I believe it helps too, to list what you are supplying; rather like a covering invoice: "Novel — fantasy — *Bug-eyed in Balawi*, by Gordon Wells; 90,000 words in 10 chapters on 442 sheets of MS, plus six sheets of prelims." This takes no time to do, but is a useful record.

- If the book is illustrated, do not on any account stick the pictures in the relevant pages in the MS, nor leave space for them. At the very most, mark preferred illustration locations in the left margin, in pencil.

- Again, for a non-fiction book with headings and sub-headings, mark the heading "weight" in pencil in the left margin; thus, main headings mark "A", sub-headings mark "B" — as a means of differentiation.

- Almost inevitably, you will make the odd mistake in the MS and wish to correct it before despatch. This is perfectly acceptable if there are not too many small corrections or alterations. If too many, do a partial retype. Make alterations clearly and positively: strike through the wrong words and write the correction in the space above it; do not write over the wrong words. And keep out of the margins — they are for the publisher's use.

- If you need to insert a whole new MS page, number the new page (say) 99A; at the foot of page 99, write "99A follows", at the foot of page 99A, write "100 follows". If you take pages out make similar notes: at the foot of page 97 write "100 follows" to indicate that pages 98 and 99 have been deleted.

5

From Typescript to Bookseller

Your book has been accepted. You're over the moon. You look forward to seeing it in print, in the bookshops. You've done your job, now it's all downhill.

Well not quite. There is much that has to be done between delivery and publication. Not all of it requires your attention but all deserves your interest.

Whether you have written a novel or a non-fiction book, your manuscript will be read, and worked on, by two different editors — who may be the same person. First comes what is sometimes called the commissioning editor, whose job is to ensure that the book as a whole makes sense. This editor checks that you haven't left a sub-plot dangling, that you have explained all you need to explain — basically, that the book *reads* well.

As a result of the commissioning editor's work, you may be asked to add in a page or two of explanation or to rearrange a sequence.

If you have quoted at any length from the work of other writers, the editor will wish to see their written permission — or will help you to obtain it. You may have to pay for the right to quote. If for any reason, you cannot get such permission, you will need to adjust your text to leave out the unauthorised quotation.

With some publishers, the payment of the "on delivery" element of the advance is not paid until you have satisfied all the commissioning editor's requirements.

The other editorial task is what is called copy-editing. It is usually combined with page layout and design. Copy-editors check your punctuation, your spelling, and your grammar. It is the nature of things that copy-editors are fussy perfectionists. And some authors are . . . well, sometimes just a wee bit slap-dash about such matters.

A copy-editor will adjust your manuscript to fit the publisher's *house style* — single or double quote marks, the use of *-ise* or *-ize* spelling, etc. Your paragraph indents will also need to be adjusted: most writers indent every paragraph with a consistent five spaces; in print, opening paragraphs, those following headings, and those after a "pause space", are not indented.

In some non-fiction books, particularly in the "how to" type of books I usually write, key points are often listed; it is a very good presentational method. I like to identify each point in the list with a *blob* (sometimes called a *bullet*) — a large black dot. In typescript, I use a lower case O with the centre inked in, and then start the text after a two-character space.

The copy/layout editor ensures that the printer uses a correct and (consistent) *bullet* and indent, and that a suitable space is left above and below the list.

Another part of the layout process is to tell the printer the type to be used for chapter and other headings. This is usually done by writing "Chapter" and "A", "B", etc., in the margin alongside the heading; such instructions are ringed, to differentiate them from textual corrections.

Most publishers will show the author the edited typescript before it now goes to typesetting. A minor editorial alteration could inadvertently have changed the meaning. More often, the changes are for the best.

Any authorial check on such an edited typescript has to be done very quickly; I have often done it in the publisher's office in an hour or so. There's always a mad rush at this stage.

While the editing process has been proceeding, other parts of the publishing organisation have also been working on your book. Someone will have drafted the text for the back cover. Earlier, you will have been asked to provide material for this *blurb*. Many non-fiction publishers ask you to complete a long questionnaire, others just ask for a 50-word biography.

The back cover text is one of the most important parts of the whole book. It's part of the sales pitch. It has to sell the book, quickly, to the casual "picker-up". You will usually be shown the back cover text; don't try to restyle it, just make any essential factual corrections.

A little later, you *ought* to see the proof of the book's cover. But you might get forgotten. And you won't really have much say in it. (I got a bit upset once, when not only was my name wrong, but an essential apostrophe was omitted. This was unusual though, and was very quickly corrected.)

One day, out of the blue, a large package will arrive at your door. No, not the finished book. This time it will be the proofs, hopefully, but not always, accompanied by the edited typescript.

In the past, proofs were often in two stages — galley proofs (long sheets of typeset work not divided into page-lengths) and then, later, page proofs. Nowadays it is more usual to get page proofs only — to "go straight to page proof". You will also often get a scribbled note asking for the speedy return of the corrected proofs. Once again, you will be under pressure to work very quickly.

There are standard symbols for use in correcting proofs. It is helpful if you work to the standard. But it is more important that you make your comments or suggested alterations very clear. Your copy of the corrected proofs goes back to the editor who collates your comments with his/her own before passing them on to the printer.

It is most important that you use the proofs only to *correct* typesetting errors — *not* to redraft the book. Don't believe all those stories about famous authors virtually rewriting their books at proof stage. You certainly can't do this nowadays. Every change you make costs a disproportionate amount of money; if you make too many changes, as opposed to corrections of typesetting errors, you will be charged with the cost. (Read the small print in your contract.)

When checking the proofs watch out particularly for repeated lines or

126

for whole lines missed out. (The typesetter takes a tea break and restarts at the wrong line.) Then send the corrected proofs back.

If the book is a non-fiction one, you may have to produce an index. You can't complete that without the page proofs — but now, as always, it is wanted quickly.

(I like to make sure that any delays in production are the fault of the publisher, and not mine. Then I can complain when something goes wrong and the book is delayed. It will. And my moaning won't help, but it makes me feel better.)

Sometime while the book is being typeset, the publisher will produce an Advance Information sheet (sometimes called the AI sheet). This tells the sales team and, through them, the booksellers, what the book is about and why it is important. You will seldom see this AI sheet but it can be quite interesting.

Surprisingly soon after you have corrected the proofs, the book will be printed. Your publisher will have printed copies about six weeks before publication date. This advance delivery is supposedly to ensure that copies of the books will be in the shops on publication day. You may get your own copies early too.

Now you wait agog for publication day. Don't expect a champagne book-launch party; don't expect to be on Wogan; don't expect a review in the *Sunday Courier*. Publication day will be awfully flat. Few will even notice the appearance of the world's latest bestseller-to-be. You just might get a congratulations telegram — but it'll more likely be from your mother.

If you're lucky though, your publisher's publicity department will get you one or two radio interviews. Probably only on local radio.

Anyway, congratulations. You're a published author at last. Now get back to work, on the next book.

NOTE: This chapter first appeared as a shorter article in *Freelance Writing & Photography*.

6

Word Processing for Book Writers

It used to be said that when writers got together they talked only about their publishers, their agents . . . and money. Today, they also talk about their word processors — usually their Amstrads. And they usually mean the Amstrad PCW8256, the PCW8512, or the PCW9512 — hereafter referred to collectively as the PCW (there are many other Amstrad computers).

But just what is a word processor? The name has come to mean the full set of equipment whereby the user can type at a standard keyboard, see the resultant words instantly on a screen before his/her eyes, amend and corrent them at will, store (and retrieve) them electronically, and then print them onto paper as and when necessary. But the equipment is really a computer (plus a printer) capable of several other uses; and the word processor itself is just a set of electronic instructions to the computer.

The concept of word processing is more easily accepted if the equipment itself is understood. Every word processor consists of the same items:

- a computer
- a keyboard
- a monitor
- a storage device
- a printer
- a word processor.

Although many people buy their word processor as a complete package (the PCW), it is quite possible to buy the various items separately. Indeed, this is essential if better equipment is wanted. There can be problems with linking together different pieces of equipment though — its built-in compatibility is one of the major advantages of the PCW — but nowadays, advice is not too hard to find.

To piece the equipment together, it helps to know what each item does, and a little bit of the "how".

The Computer

A computer — the *central processing unit* or CPU — handles instructions and information as a collection of "on" or "off" notifications. Think of millions of switches; each can be either on or off. A computer "reads" each item of information in the form of eight switch-instructions; each number, each letter, and each punctuation mark can be expressed in a sequence of eight ons and offs (usually thought of as 0s and 1s, in *binary* code). Each 8-digit item of information is called a *byte*.

A computer has a memory: all those millions of switches. The size of its memory is measured in bytes (sets of eight switches) — or, more usually in thousands of bytes, known as *kilobytes*, or just K. The Amstrad PCW9512 has a built-in memory (sometimes called RAM, meaning Random Access Memory) of 512 kilobytes, 512K — hence the model number, (9)512.

As we are only really interested in the computer's word-processing ability, we could translate that memory size of 512,000 bytes into roughly 60,000 ordinary everyday words — and the space around them. But some part of the computer's memory (its RAM) is used to hold its program of instructions. Allowing for the program, you may well have room for only 30–40,000 words — but this is quite enough. You need hold no more in memory than just what you are working on immediately. You don't need the whole book in memory.

When you stop work — and also, for safety, at intervals whilst working — you will "save" your electronic work onto disks (*see below*). Once saved, your work cannot be lost by the computer — although of course the disks could be physically destroyed or lost.

The Keyboard

To be able to feed information into your computer you need a keyboard on which to type. A computer keyboard is precisely the same as a normal QWERTY typewriter keyboard. (QWERTY because of the sequence of the first six keys in the top line of letters.) But computers need extra keys. Every computer keyboard however will have the all-important *Enter* key, a delete key or keys, and a means of moving the cursor (*see below*) around the screen. There are other keys but they will vary from machine to machine.

The Enter key — which could initially be confused with the conventional typewriter's new-line key — is used to activate instructions to the computer and at paragraph ends. With a word processor you need never again worry about the end of the line; the computer reads your input as a series of paragraph-length lines which it then displays on the screen as normal typescript. You set the margins you want, and the computer moves your words on, from line to line, automatically.

The Monitor

Just like a television screen, a computer monitor displays the action. Before you start to type the screen will display what is called the *cursor*. The appearance of the cursor will vary but it is often a small upright oblong, the size of one typed character. The cursor tells you where your typing will appear on the screen. Touch any key. The initial cursor position will be taken up by the character you keyed in, and the cursor will have moved one space to the right. Continue, and you form a word on screen.

Monitors can have green, amber, black and white, or multi-colour screens. Some writers find a multi-colour word-processing screen rather distracting. Certainly, monochrome screens are cheaper.

The monitor screen will not only display the words you type; it will also carry, at the very least, what is called a *status line*. On my own (non-PCW) screen the status line tells me which page I am working on, which line on that page, and how many words I have written in a particular document. Other status lines are less or more useful. It is also possible, on my set-up, to call up on-screen advice on the word processor program.

The Storage

As mentioned above, the work you put into your word processor computer must be saved before you stop work — and also at more frequent intervals to prevent accidental loss. The program allows you to do this. But you need a storage device. Today, this storage is almost universally one or more disk drives.

You can have a single disk drive, from which the program is read in, and out to which the work is saved; you can have a pair of drives, one of which is usually used for the program and the other for saving onto; or you can have what is called a hard disk drive plus a single (floppy) disk drive. This latter set-up lets you hold your program permanently within the computer on the large capacity fast-access hard disk; you save your own work onto the same disk; you can make extra, safety-first, copies onto an ordinary floppy disk on the other drive.

Computer/word processing storage is like recording music onto a cassette. You insert a blank disk and record your new work onto it; next day, you play it back, make corrections, and re-record it. And you can buy ready-made disks — the program — which you use in your work. The words you write onto the screen are recorded onto the disks in the form of electronic "blips" (representing ons and offs, or 0s and 1s).

The disks used for storage come in various sizes. The PCW uses special 3-inch disks; the latest computers use 3.5-inch disks; older models use 5.25-inch disks known as "floppies" — because they are. All of these disks are removable from the machine and are stored separately. The hard disk mentioned above is installed permanently in the computer; it is not removable. In all cases though, including the hard disk, once work is saved to a disk it is as safe as any audio-cassette recording. The computer can be switched off without fear of loss.

The Printer

It is all very fine composing your thoughts onto a monitor screen, via a keyboard, and then saving them onto disks. Eventually, even in these

130

electronic days, you will still need to produce words on paper. And that means you need a printer.

Computer printers come in three types, laser, daisy-wheel, and dot-matrix. The laser printer turns out work of exceptionally high quality, much like a photocopying machine. But although the cost of a laser printer is falling sharply, it is still over £1,000 and hardly justified for most writers — unless you want to go in for self-publishing in a big way. Most writers will choose between a daisy-wheel and a dot-matrix printer.

A daisy-wheel printer operates in much the same way as a typewriter — certainly as an electronic typewriter. Individual characters are moulded on the ends of thin arms fixed to a central hub. It is called a daisy-wheel because it is thought to look like a daisy.

The daisy-wheel spins under instructions from the computer to place the appropriate character directly in front of the next space on the paper. A tiny hammer strikes the wheels' arm onto an inked ribbon which hits the paper and marks it with the required symbol.

The quality of typescript produced with a daisy-wheel printer is identical with that produced on an electronic typewriter. There is however a limit to the speed at which a daisy-wheel printer can operate — few print faster than a claimed 50 characters per second, and most reasonable-priced models manage no more than 20 characters per second. (Allowing for line-end turnrounds, the more affordable printers will take 2–3 minutes to print an A4 page of double-spaced typescript.)

A dot-matrix printer works in a completely different way. A row of fine pins project from a printing head. As each character is needed, the computer program instructs the print head which pins are to project out against the inked ribbon and onto the page. Each character is made up of several upright rows of pin marks — dots. Early dot-matrix printers used nine pins in a matrix 7 or 9 rows wide. The characters so formed were universally "dotty", but the machines operated fast.

To improve the quality of dot-matrix printing some machines offer a double run of the printing head. On the second run, the head is slightly displaced from its original position and the pin marks fill in the gaps left on the first run. This is known as near letter quality (NLQ) printing. The quality is variable, but usually quite good; it is readily distinguishable from daisy-wheel printing though. NLQ printing on a dot-matrix printer is almost as slow as daisy-wheel printing; but the printer produces drafts very quickly.

In the past, writers were always advised to avoid dot-matrix printers; publishers, editors and printers universally disliked the "dotty" type-scripts. But now there are 24-pin dot-matrix printers, with exceptional print quality. The 24-pin printers operate in a single pass with very fine pins much closer together than the older machines (24 dots in the space of the earlier 9). Their output is virtually indistinguishable from that of a daisy-wheel and it is much faster; and they retain the facility for very fast draft printing. (My own Star 24-pin printer produces excellent typescript at 60 characters per second — well under a minute for an A4 page of double-spaced manuscript — and draft output at a staggering 180 characters per second.) I would recommend a 24-pin dot-matrix printer to any writer.

The Word Processor

All of the equipment however — in computer jargon, the "hardware" — is only as good as the instructions which make it work. The instructions are in the program, otherwise known as the "software". (The PCW provides Locoscript. It takes a bit of learning but once you are used to it, it is very "powerful" — more computer jargon for "you can do a lot of different things with it".)

If you have grown used to the PCW you do not need to consider the program to use, you have one. But if you are looking for a bigger, more robust set of equipment, you will need to think about the word processor program. There are many programs available offering a variety of different facilities. Try looking at the computer press — or consulting a dealer.

My own favourite, getting a bit "long-in-the-tooth" but which I have not yet been able to fault, is a program called Quill, which is part of PSION's integrated PC-FOUR suite.

When investigating the purchase of a separate word processor program, it is helpful to know what facilities can be available and which are most useful to a writer. In my view, a writer's word processor should offer:

- WYSIWYG — meaning *what you see is what you get*, and nowadays almost universally available.

- The ability to insert, remove or transfer words, phrases or paragraphs anywhere within the document which is then readily (or better, automatically) reformatted.

- A facility for changing margins at will, anywhere within a document.

- The ability to draft, and print out, in single-spaced typing, and then, for a final MS, readily to change to double-spaced typescript.

- The ability to write a *file* (jargon for a document) of up to say 5,000 words (45K) length and to move from one end of the document to the other without delay.

- A "search and replace" facility. You name a character Bill throughout your book; you decide to rename him John; "search and replace" lets you do this quickly and automatically, file by file, with just a very few simple instructions.

- A "macro" or "glossary" feature that will let you produce commonly-used phrases, addresses, etc. on screen with one or two keystrokes. (When I key in F5–G for instance, my word processor instantly brings up my full name and address.)

- An ability to store, and call up as necessary, various page layouts — eg, for articles and books, or for letters.

132

- An on-screen rolling word count. I couldn't live without it.

- A built-in spelling checker. At the end of a document, you should be able to call up a check on the spelling — and be offered suggestions for corrections or be able to incorporate your own new words.

- An on-screen indication of the end of each page — and the ability to force a page-ending at will.

- The ability to merge files together — for instance, to add more material to the end of a chapter by incorporating part of another file (a part-chapter from another book perhaps).

- The ability to print individual pages from within a multi-page document.

Most word processor programs will offer most of the above facilities; before selecting a program you must check which are of most importance to you and which you can sacrifice for some other benefit. But most programs are very good.

7

Miscellany

A book writer's life is more than mere words, word processors and market research. There is a whole wide world beyond the figments of their imagination or their favoured non-fiction subjects. In this chapter we look at some aspects of that world.

Trade Unions

Any book writer can benefit from joining the Society of Authors. The Society looks after the interests of writers in general and its 5,000 members in particular. It is an independent trade union. It is not affiliated to the TUC or to any political party.

You can only become a member once you have a full-length book published — or at least accepted for publication. If you have had a number of short stories or articles published, you can however be considered for Associate Membership of the Society. And while you are still seeking publication, you can subscribe to the Society's quarterly magazine *The Author*; at around £18 per annum it is a worthwhile investment.

But what can the Society of Authors do for you? It provides members with informed advice about agents and publishers; it offers experienced and professional advice on contractual negotiations with agents or publishers, and it will scrupulously vet any contract you are offered; it will, in certain circumstances, provide massive legal support to members; it negotiates better terms and conditions for all writers; and it regularly promulgates advice and information on matters of interests to the writing world. It enables writers to negotiate on general matters from the strength of union.

Membership of the Society of Authors costs £50 per annum. Full information from The Society of Authors, 84 Drayton Gardens, London SW10 9SB, or telephone 071–373 6642.

Whereas the Society of Authors is concerned mainly with book-writers, The Writers' Guild of Great Britain is more concerned with representing the interests of writers in the film, TV, radio and stage fields. But this differentiation is not rigid; there are book-writers in the Guild and scriptwriters in the Society. Although the Guild is TUC-affiliated, it has no involvement with any political party and its members pay no political levy.

The Writers' Guild offers much the same sort of services as does the Society but inevitably with more emphasis on the concerns of the film, TV, radio and stage writer. Membership requirements are based on a points system: publication of a full-length book or production of an hour-long film or play carries enough points for full membership; shorter works are aggregated until there are sufficient. Subscriptions are based on a percentage of writing earnings with upper and lower limits.

Write for further details, to The Writers' Guild of Great Britain, 430 Edgware Road, London W2 1EH, or telephone 071–723 8074.

Clubs, Workshops and Conferences

Ideal for sharing problems, learning new techniques, and celebrating successes with other writers, there are writing circles or clubs all over Great Britain — and indeed in many places throughout the world. Ask at local libraries or adult education centres for details. (Many writers' circles have grown out of evening classes in writing.)

At the least, such clubs offer companionship in what is otherwise a lonely occupation. At the best, dependent on the knowledge and experience of other members and the quality of visiting speakers, they can be real hothouses for the development of new talents. Investigate your local writing club for yourself. Bask in the friendship, warmth and particularly the criticism of experienced writers; but flee the uncritical tea-party world of inexperienced mutual adulation.

Many writing clubs offer a programme of regular workshops. Customarily, workshop participants read their work aloud to others; it is then criticised, but always constructively, by all, or by the workshop leader. Again, depending on the workshop leader, this can be invaluable — or totally destructive. Find out who people are before taking their advice.

There are other opportunities for workshop help. Some writing circles run one-day conferences incorporating workshop sessions. Leaders of such workshops will almost always be worth listening to. Watch the writing press for details of "open" writing workshops.

And then there are the writing conferences. There are two week-long conferences: the long-established Writers' Summer School — known to all as "Swanwick", after the town in Derbyshire where it is held each August; and the newer Writers' Holiday held at Caerleon in Wales each July (with a mini-holiday too at Easter). Other well-established writers "get-togethers" are the weekends: the Southern Writers Conference at Chichester (a super weekend in mid-June), the Scarborough weekends (in April and November), and the Cardiff SAMWAW weekends (in May and September).

Addresses to write to — always remembering to send a stamped self-addressed envelope — for information about these conferences are:

- Swanwick: Philippa Boland, The Red House, Mardens Hill, Crowborough, East Sussex TN6 1XN.

- Caerleon: D. L. Anne Hobbs, 30 Pant Road, Newport, Gwent NP9 5PR.

- Southern: Ann Hutton, Trevenen House, 44 Esplanade, Fowey, Cornwall PL23 1HZ.

- Scarborough: Audrey Wilson, The Firs, Filey Road, Osgodby, Scarborough, North Yorks YO11 3NH.

- Cardiff: Muriel Ross, 129 Carisbrooke Way, Cyncoed, Cardiff CF3 7HU.

Each conference has a spirit of its own but all are enjoyable and offer valuable advice and/or instruction. Not only that, but you will make social contact with other writers which can blossom into really permanent friendships. And you can talk shop — or listen to it — all day long.

As well as the weekend and week-long conferences, there are many one-day writers' get-togethers organised by individual writers' circles. Among the better annual meetings of which I know are the West Sussex Writers' Day at Worthing, Freelance Press Services' Days at Eccles near Manchester, the local Writers' Circle Day at Southport, and Ivy McKnight's Northavon Writers' Seminar at Chipping Sodbury. There are many others.

The Society of Authors organises occasional weekend conferences, usually quite small, usually on specific themes. These are announced well in advance in the Society's magazine *The Author*.

You may think that writers' conferences are not for you; you can't stand people *en masse*; you are afraid that you won't know anyone. These worries are understandable; some people do not enjoy these shindigs; but you needn't worry about not knowing anyone — you will always be made welcome. I can only say that I wrote for 30 years without knowing — or realizing I was missing — the company of other writers. Then I went to my first weekend conference and got hooked. Now I can't understand how I survived without them. Do try one.

Books on Writing

Books on writing abound. Like writing circles, the quality of the advice will depend on the ability and experience of the author. Grouped by the type of book to which they relate, I have found the following books — relating solely to book-writing — helpful:

General fiction:

Writing a Novel, John Braine, Eyre Methuen, 1974.
One Way to Write a Novel, Dick Winfield, Writer's Digest (US), 1969.
The Craft of Novel-Writing, Dianne Doubtfire, Allison & Busby, 1978.
The Making of a Novelist, Margaret Thomson Davis, Allison & Busby, 1982.
Writing Historical Fiction, Rhona Martin, A. & C. Black, 1988.
How to Write Historical Fiction, Michael Legat, Allison & Busby, 1990.

Romance:

To Writers With Love, Mary Wibberley, Buchan & Enright, 1985.
The Craft of Writing Romance, Jean Saunders, Allison & Busby, 1986.

Crime/Suspense/Thriller:

Writing a Thriller, André Jute, A. & C. Black, 1986.
Writing Crime Fiction, H. R. F. Keating, A. & C. Black, 1986.

Non-fiction:

The Successful Author's Handbook, Gordon Wells, Papermac, 2/e 1989.

There are of course, many more books on how to write. All I have done is list the books about book-writing that I have read, and enjoyed or found useful. I have deliberately omitted the several excellent books on general creative writing; if you are reading this book, you are past the need for such guidance.

Public Lending Right (PLR)

The main sources of a writer's income from writing are the royalties paid on copies sold, and the advance against these royalties. But the public does not only *buy* books — indeed, the British are not great book-buyers at all. Many people borrow their reading matter from the public libraries. Until Public Lending Right was introduced in 1980 the author received just a single royalty fee for a library book, on its purchase. Now, a registered author is paid a small sum per loan, currently around a penny, from public funds.

As soon as your first book is published (but not before), you should register yourself and the book with the Registrar of Public Lending Right. Write to The Registrar, PLR Office, Bayheath House, Prince Regent Street, Stockton-on-Tees, Cleveland TS18 1DF for registration application forms and full details.

Do not expect to earn a fortune from PLR. You only get about a penny per loan. In all, there are roughly 17,500 registered authors: just under 10,000 receive between £1 and £100; over 3,000 others get nothing at all. PLR payments are restricted to not more than £6000 to any registered author; less than 30 authors were in that category in 1989/90. But even if you only get £5 in PLR, this is £5 more than you would otherwise get; it is always worth registering.

Every penny is worth picking up. Very few writers get rich from their writing alone. But it's a great way to go.